RICE UNIVERSITY

SEMICENTENNIAL PUBLICATIONS

The Nation's
Economic Objectives

EDITOR

EDGAR O. EDWARDS

CONTRIBUTORS

KENNETH E. BOULDING

ARTHUR F. BURNS

LESTER V. CHANDLER

SEYMOUR E. HARRIS

SIMON KUZNETS

FRITZ MACHLUP

EDWARD S. MASON

JACOB VINER

The Nation's

Economic

Objectives

E. O. Edwards

PUBLISHED FOR

WILLIAM MARSH RICE UNIVERSITY

BY

THE UNIVERSITY OF CHICAGO PRESS

Library of Congress Catalog Card Number: 64-15816

THE UNIVERSITY OF CHICAGO PRESS, CHICAGO & LONDON
The University of Toronto Press, Toronto 5, Canada

Preface

Authors such as those represented in this volume need no introduction to economists, and a sampling of their wares will convince the layman that he has access through these essays to a group of singularly knowledgeable people. Whether economist or layman, the reader may disagree with some of the evaluations he finds here, but it is likely, too, that he will find others to support his own. In any event intellectual stimulation must depend on new ideas and on this score no reader should be disappointed.

The book brings together original appraisals by several leading economists in the United States of this nation's important economic objectives—what they are, how they originated and grew, and the conditions necessary to their achievement. These assessments are made at a time when the nation's objectives are being subjected to searching examination by both professional people and informed citizens. At no time in the past have the aims of this society been more deeply or more widely discussed and constructively criticized. The carefully presented, well-documented analyses published in this book should stimulate clear and objective thinking on subjects which will dominate executive and legislative economic decisions for many years ahead.

It would be both foolhardy and presumptuous for an editor to attempt to summarize the varied insights and rich content of these essays. They deal with a wide range of national goals, including economic growth, full employment, stability, international adjustment, social and economic security, economic freedom, and the role of public policy. The reader will find fresh and revealing evidence on the historical pattern of United States growth and how this compares with patterns in other countries; the full-employment problem is analyzed with new perspective; economic freedom emerges with unusual and challenging dimensions; the record of international co-operation is both revealing and instructive; and the view of the United States as a "welfare state" may astonish some readers but will certainly stimulate all.

While it is the economic objectives of the United States that supply a common focus to these articles, there are frequent comparisons with experiences in other countries. At a time when underdeveloped and newly independent countries are attempting to define economic policy objectives of their own, the experience and problems of a more advanced country may prove to be a valuable record both of things to avoid and of things to imitate. Other advanced countries may find United States experience to be more directly applicable, and for that reason even more revealing.

It should perhaps be stressed in this era when reprinting is fashionable that these are original works written expressly for this book and the occasion it represents. The semicentennial anniversary of Rice University was suitably celebrated by a variety of scholarly works of which this is one. In the field of economics an analysis of national objectives, their roots and problems of achievement, seemed especially appropriate to mark the fiftieth birthday of a university devoted to the nation's welfare and itself in the midst of serious study of its past progress and future aims. Each of the authors was invited to give a lecture at Rice University during the academic year 1962–63, and it is these on which the articles included in this volume are based.

As editor of the volume I want to record here my pleasure in working with the authors; their excellent and painstaking work made my task a simple one. It is a great injustice to each of them that this book is catalogued under my name. I should also like to thank Mrs. Mildred Pegues for her secretarial assistance.

EDGAR O. EDWARDS

Contents

EDWARD S. MASON

Objectives of a Mature Society

MATURITY is a slippery concept to handle not only as it applies to human growth but particularly as it applies to the growth of societies. It obviously possesses strong value connotations, some favorable and others unfavorable. All of us want to be mature in the sense that we have acquired a fully developed personality and a set of faculties. But despite Rabbi ben Ezra and a number of other sages, very few of us glory in that stage of maturity that is close to decay. I suppose that is one reason why, just as most Americans whatever their income group think of themselves as middle class, many of us, even in the seventh decade of life (as I am), still consider ourselves as middle-aged. Ripeness is *not* all; there is such a thing as being too ripe.

Toynbee, among others, has accustomed us to think also of civilizations in terms of a life cycle. All past societies known to man have experienced growth, maturity, and decay. I would presume that in some sense and over some period what we call "Western capitalist" or "Western industrial" society will go through the same cycle. But it is difficult, if not impossible, for any one to diagnose with respect to his own society the degree of arteriosclerosis to which at any particular time it is subject. And attempts to do so tend, on the whole, not to be kindly received. In the late 1930's the term "economic maturity" became popular among some economists, and it was identified with an alleged inability of a high-income, free-enterprise economy to generate sufficient investment opportunities to absorb the volume of savings such an economy tends to accumulate. One would have to say, I think, in the light of our unsatisfactory growth rate during the last five or six years that the arguments of this group of economists have not yet been completely answered. But I do not propose to make myself the target of flying brickbats and dead cats by espousing this particular definition of maturity here.

EDWARD S. MASON is Thomas W. Lamont University Professor at Harvard and teaches Economics.

1

For my purposes maturity means nothing more than a high level of per capita income, and my concern is with some of the domestic problems that arise from the changing structure of wants and activities that accompanies growth in per capita income. I propose to take stability and growth for granted and to ask what tends to happen to patterns of demand and resource use in a high-income economy that maintains something like full employment and a substantial growth rate. Recent historical trends tell us something about what we may expect and foreshadow some of the problems we are likely to face. In particular I am interested in the question whether the relations between government and the increasingly well-organized interest groups that constitute so important a part of our society are sufficiently flexible to permit a satisfactory adjustment to these changing wants and activities. The capacity to adjust to the volume and type of technological changes that confront us over the next quarter century and to the impending shifts in demand is not only a necessary condition for the maintenance of growth in output but also to the assurance that the output of which we are capable is adapted to the objectives of a mature society.

Such adaptation requires social change and institutional innovation, and recent experience suggests how much easier it appears to be to manipulate the physical world than to make even moderate changes in the way of life of people and of societies. A Telstar is put into orbit with little fuss and bother, but though the farm problem has been with us for a long time it appears to be no nearer solution than it was a decade ago. Spacemen chase each other around the world like fox and rabbit, but serious unemployment persists indefinitely in a number of depressed areas. It seems probable that we shall land a man on the moon before we succeed in making a dent in the traffic problem around Grand Central Station. Yet institutional invention holds out more promise for the well-being of the people of the United States over the foreseeable future than anything the spacemen can do for us.

Certain of the economic problems that at the moment seem most pressing would most certainly disappear if we could succeed in sustaining something like full employment over a reasonable period of time. And this does not seem to be beyond the wit of man when one considers that a number of western European countries with economic and social institutions not very different from ours have done so while maintaining a growth rate at least double that we have been able to achieve over the last five years. The essential difference seems to be that an adequate set of stabilization policies is regarded by all important interests in Europe as a conservative alternative to a more extreme degree of government intervention, while in this country we have never been quite willing to accept the implications and responsibilities of the Employment Act of 1946.

The point to be emphasized is that certain of the economic problems that have plagued us persistently since World War II are not the deep-seated consequences of structural maladjustment. They could be expected to yield quite easily to the application of sensible fiscal and monetary policy. In this category I would put both the farm problem and the issue of distressed areas. Nor am I much worried about the alleged effects of automation on employment opportunities.

Despite the fact that the net migration from farms has gone on steadily for half a century, reached its high point in the decade of the forties and was only a little less striking in the fifties, there are still nearly two million too many farm people in the United States. It can be confidently expected that the rate of increase in man-hour production in agriculture will continue to be high, and equally confidently it can be expected that the rate of increase in the demand for farm products will be low. In the meantime we shall no doubt continue to spend $4 or $5 billion a year to support farm prices, to store surplus crops, and to sell abroad for inconvertible currencies whatever amount we can dispose of in that way. The price-support program no doubt holds on the farm surplus workers who would otherwise move, but the most important reason they do not move is that jobs outside of farming are not opening up fast enough to absorb them. Despite the effects of price supports the incomes of a large fraction of farmers are still lower than those they could expect to get in urban employment. The decade of the forties was supposedly a heyday for farmers, but heydey or no the net migration off the farms in that decade was the largest in our history. The reason obviously was that urban jobs were available. Ten years of full employment, if they would not eliminate the farm problem entirely, would reduce it to a size not worth serious consideration.

Another problem that has plagued both the Eisenhower and Kennedy administrations and, in the absence of adequate stabilization policies, is likely to be with us for a long time is the existence of so-called distressed areas, where more than average rates of unemployment tend to persist over long periods. Areas of this sort exist in almost all parts of the country, and unemployment rates of 15 per cent are not uncommon. In some quarters it is feared that the international trade program on which we are embarked will increase the numbers of and worsen the conditions in these areas. This is one aspect of so-called structural unemployment which is said also to affect certain racial and age groups with particular severity and to be accentuated by technological changes that make traditional skills obsolete. That there is such a thing as structural unemployment which is relatively unresponsive to increases in aggregate demand, I would not doubt. Training programs and other policies designed to increase interindustrial and interregional mobility are useful and necessary. But recent investigations have indicated quite clearly that during the period from 1957 to date, when unemployment in the United States never fell below 4 per cent, the shortage of jobs was by no means limited to particular areas or industries. In the 1959–60 recession, according to a report of the congressional Joint Economic Committee, "Unemployment rose among workers attached to every occupational and industrial group. The rise in unemployment was particularly sharp among unexperienced workers, the group subject to the fewest wage and mobility constraints."[1]

A particularly alarming prospect of structural unemployment is presented by certain writers on the subject of automation. If they are to be believed, the machine directed by the electronic computer is about to take over, and no policies, stabilization or otherwise, can be expected to sustain employment for more than a fraction of the labor force. It does seem probable, on the basis of evidence already in, that machine techniques directed by computers are bringing and will bring a revolution in production processes beyond anything experienced since the beginning of the Industrial Revolution. But there remains, on the one hand, the practical insatiability of human wants and, on the other, the law of comparative advantage. Despite the assertions of my colleague Galbraith, the marginal utility of private expenditures has not yet fallen to zero nor is it likely to do so.[2] And although computers can do many things, they cannot do everything. Human employment, so far as one can tell, will continue to occupy a large area in which it enjoys a comparative advantage. Automation can have a revolutionary effect on the distribution of employment among various occupations without significantly affecting the total volume of employment. Automation will be likely to open up a new frontier of choice between leisure and work that we shall want to explore, but so far as one can see, work versus leisure will still be a matter of choice and not something forced on us by irremovable structural impediments to full employment.

A number, then, of the economic problems that engage serious attention can be expected to yield to sensible stabilization policy.

[1] Joint Economic Committee, Subcommittee on Economic Statistics, *Higher Unemployment Rates, 1957–60: Structural Transformation or Inadequate Demand* (Washington, D.C.: Government Printing Office, 1961), p. 78.

[2] J. K. Galbraith, *The Affluent Society* (Boston: Houghton Mifflin Co., 1958).

Furthermore, although I do not have time or space to argue the matter here, the supposed inflationary and balance-of-payments limitations to an effective stabilization policy seem to me to be greatly exaggerated. I should like to turn now to a series of problems that cannot be expected to yield to full employment. Let us then assume full employment and the rate of growth of which this country is capable at full employment, and ask what next.

Some of the important problems of a mature, high-income, high-growth-rate economy that full employment cannot be expected to solve are associated with changes in the geographical location of jobs and people, with changes in the age distribution of the population, in the distribution of consumer expenditures, and in the choice between work and leisure. A substantial part of the burden of adjustment to change can be expected to be carried by normal market responses to changing profit opportunities. But a satisfactory solution will require, I believe, the assumption of added responsibilities by government and changes in what have been traditional government-business relations in this country.

As everyone knows, the population of the United States is a highly mobile one both geographically and sociologically speaking. It will need to continue to be mobile if proper adaptation is to be made to changing job opportunities. The geographical redistribution of people during the last three or four decades has been remarkable. This in itself creates problems both for the areas of relative growth and for those of relative decline. But I am not here primarily concerned with the superior attractions of Texas, California, and Florida but with the continuing movement of population to metropolitan areas in all parts of the country.

The trek from farms to towns and cities is, of course, as old as our country. The Word War I lament, "How're You Going to Keep Them Down on the Farm," is of universal application. But the movement is not only from country to towns but from towns to cities and from smaller cities to larger ones. The metropolitan centers in almost all regions of the country have been growing somewhat faster than the regions themselves. In 1960, 63 per cent of our people lived in what the Census calls "standard metropolitan areas," and in 1980, if present trends continue, the figure will be close to 70 per cent. A recent study of the New York metropolitan area, with which I had some connection, predicts a population in 1985 of over twenty million in the area that now holds sixteen million.[3]

If close to three-quarters of our people are destined to live in

[3] Robert H. Connery and Richard H. Leach, *The Federal Government and Metropolitan Areas* (Cambridge, Mass.: Harvard University Press, 1960).

metropolitan areas and over a third in metropolises of more than a million, it is clear that their well-being will be greatly affected by what happens to our cities. And American cities, to speak bluntly but truthfully, are a mess. Nowhere in Europe or Latin America have I seen city streets as dirty or uncared for as in the typical American city. One has to go to Calcutta, Djakarta, Karachi, or some other southern Asian metropolis to find their equal. The central cities of most American metropolitan areas are losing population, and large sections of the center and its immediate surroundings are in process of decay. Minority groups account for an increasing percentage of the population of most central cities, and these groups are almost invariably ill housed. This obviously has something to do with the mounting delinquency rates.

Parks and open spaces occupy generally a smaller percentage of the settled areas than in European and Latin American cities. Little has been done to reclaim water fronts. The historic Charles River, which separates Boston and Cambridge, on which I attempt to row from time to time, is at certain seasons of the year little more than an open sewer. And this is true of the rivers in most American cities. In an attempt to escape from the increasing urban blight, the well-to-do citizenry move farther into the suburbs, and each suburb, limited only by the highly permissive nature of state control, protects itself against all others and against the central city by zoning and other regulations. Meanwhile, the daily journey to work lengthens, and the commuter finds himself spending a larger proportion of his waking hours battling traffic or using the increasingly inadequate public transportation facilities.

These are aspects of living that are not taken into account in the statistics on economic growth. It is quite possible for per capita incomes to increase steadily while the standard of living, in any proper sense of the term, declines. In an urban civilization the improvement of urban areas as places to live must, I think, be considered as one of the high-priority objectives of a mature society. A part of the reason for the neglect of our cities is no doubt to be accounted for by the overrepresentation of the rural population in state legislatures. The recent action by the Supreme Court may in time bring about a correction. If it does, there remains the question of how the increased power of the urban electorate is to be used.

A second set of problems that the maintenance of employment and an adequate growth rate will not automatically solve arises from the changing age distribution of the population. Currently there is a larger percentage of our population under eighteen and over sixty-five than there was twenty years ago. Consequently, a somewhat

heavier burden than normal tends to fall on the population of working age. This will presumably be alleviated as the products of the
high war and postwar birth rates move into the labor force. But the
high percentage of the population constituted by those over sixty-five
is here to stay. Since I am approaching that age myself, I may have
a more than usual interest in the subject.

Not only is the percentage of older people in the population increasing, but there is a strong tendency for this group to concentrate
in certain geographical areas. Florida and California, of course, have
been the favored locations, and in both states the effect of this migration on the state budget has led to special study of the subject. But the
problem of the aged is a country-wide problem, and it is a problem
whose solution requires public action for at least two reasons. It is
clear that because of the nature of income distribution, the low valua-
tion of future as against present wants, and other attitudes and values
generated in a free-spending society, no more than a small percentage
of people will, or perhaps can, accumulate enough to take care of
their old age. Secondly, the progressive disintegration of family relationships is such that the responsibility felt by the younger for the
older members of what used to be an extended family is decidedly
weak. A recent study by my colleague Simon Kuznets has indicated
that even in the relatively short period since the war there has been
a large increase in the percentage of lowest-income receivers accounted for by "either a semi- or fully retired, or of a broken family
unit."[4]

In the relatively short period since 1930, the percentage of the
population over sixty-five has increased from 5.4 per cent to slightly
over 8 per cent. Since medical progress has not, as yet, increased the
potential life-span but only the chance that more of us will approach
the potential, there is an upper limit to the percentage of the aged in
the population. On present prospects this limit may be as high as 10
per cent. In 1960 slightly less than one-quarter of the population over
sixty-five were still employed, and slightly more than three-quarters
were receiving their sole or major support from social security or
related programs. In 1930 over a third of the people in the same age
group were employed.

This sizable and still growing segment of the population increasingly excluded from employment and yet, by reason of medical advances, increasingly able to participate in the opportunities and tribu-
lations of life presents a series of problems to a society that has be-

[4] Simon Kuznets, "Income Distribution and Changes in Consumption," in *Report of
the Arden House Conference on the Changing American Population* (New York:
Institute of Life Insurance, 1962), p. 36.

come mature in at least two senses of the word. What share of the national income shall be allotted to this segment of the population, and how is this allotment to be financed? With the weakening of family responsibility this has become in the main a public policy decision. At present, despite social security, the lowest-income brackets are increasingly occupied by the retired. This is almost inevitably so with a retirement compensation plan that relies heavily on insurance principles in a period of persistent inflation. Yet, if admittedly inadequate incomes are to be supplemented by tax revenues, this is essentially a transfer from the working population to those who, by reason of age, have left the labor force. Such transfers have always been recognized as proper and inevitable in the extended-family system that once existed in this country and still exists in most of the underdeveloped world. With the disintegration of family relationships in a highly mobile, impersonal, self-centered, market-oriented economy, must they not become the inevitable responsibility of the state?

The problems of the aged, moreover, are by no means exclusively financial. If people over sixty-five are to be active and interested until seventy-five or eighty, in what are they going to be active and interested? The primary responsibility for finding this out obviously belongs to the individual primarily concerned. But if

> The best is yet to be,
> The last of life, for which the first was made

the individual primarily concerned will be enormously helped by private and public actions based on a recognition of the fact that while life may begin at forty, it does not end at sixty-five. Should retirement ages be increased, and if so how is that to be brought about in a society in which most job opportunities are in the hands of managements who are not generally inclined to believe that this is the best way to increase profits? Is there a community responsibility for initiating programs of useful employment, either paid or unpaid? Can the construction industry, in response to the profit motive, be relied on to provide the type and grade of housing that satisfies minimum requirements? And are the facilities necessary for taking care of the aged when they are no longer able to fend for themselves adequate? Even the most perfunctory examination suggests that the answer to these questions is "no."

The problems of the retired and the aged are not new problems, but they are problems that are new in magnitude. Furthermore, with continually increasing per capita incomes they are problems for the solution of which the material resources are available. I suggest that one of the objectives of a mature society should be adequate provision for the members who are in fact mature.

A third set of issues confronting a mature society arises from the inevitable shifts in the pattern of demand as per capita incomes rise. We are all familiar with the low income elasticity of demand for farm products which, along with the fantastic increases in agricultural productivity, explains the continuous decline in farm employment. Since 1920 agriculture's share of total employment has fallen from 18 per cent to less than 9 per cent. Less familiar but perhaps as striking are the relative stability and probable prospective decline of manufacturing employment as a percentage of total employment. The failure of the share of manufacturing employment to rise significantly during the last forty years is indicated in Table 1.

TABLE 1

PER CENT OF GAINFULLY
EMPLOYED OCCUPIED
IN MANUFACTURING

Year	Per Cent
1920	26
1930	23
1940	24
1950	25
1960	24.5

In the absence of large defense expenditures, it is probable that the per cent employed in manufacturing in 1940, 1950, and 1960 would be somewhat less than indicated in the table.

The areas of large percentage gains in employment during this period are, of course, trade, finance, government, and personal (including professional) services. All these activities belong in that highly conglomerate sector called by the Census "service industries." The service sector in the American economy is already very large as compared with European economies and accounted for slightly over 50 per cent of total employment in 1960. In some quarters this is offered as at least a partial explanation of the slow growth rate of the American economy in recent years, since a large part of the service sector is not capital intensive and offers smaller opportunities than elsewhere in the economy for productivity gains. However that may be, there appear to be good reasons for believing that the relative size of the service sector will increase rather than diminish as per capita incomes increase. The rather marked shift in consumer expenditures toward services is likely to continue; the rising share of government expenditures is predominantly in the service area, and it seems probable that as computer-guided machine processes replace workers the comparative advantage of human effort will be found largely in certain branches of the service sector.

There is no reason why the major part of these anticipated shifts in output and employment cannot be accommodated by private responses to market incentives. But in certain rapidly growing service areas, government will have to play a larger role if the objectives of a mature society are to be realized adequately. I have in mind particularly the rapid increase in the demand for education, for medical services and hospitalization, and for recreation and recreational facilities.

Whether educational outlays should be mainly regarded as capital investment or consumption expenditures is a question that does not concern us here. Properly calculated, educational costs already absorb a sizable fraction of private and public budgets, and the percentage is increasing. Public expenditures on educational plants and teachers' salaries are only the visible part of the iceberg representing total educational costs. The maintenance expenditures of families for students who are in school at ages when they could be earning account for a larger amount. And if the difference between potential earnings and maintenance charges is included as part of educational costs, the size of the iceberg becomes imposing. Furthermore, it is increasing rapidly as the school-leaving age rises.

Government has, of course, traditionally always assumed the major burden of providing the visible expenditures on education. Furthermore, it will have to increase its share as private educational institutions find financing more difficult. Government has also begun to assume some of the maintenance costs of students at the graduate level, and it will no doubt go further in this direction. That part of the egalitarian doctrine that even nineteenth-century liberalism was prepared to accept was equality of opportunity, and increasingly equality of opportunity is seen to depend largely on equality of educational preparation. Furthermore, it is coming to be realized that in the kind of competition in which the United States is engaged we cannot afford to neglect the development of such talent as is available to us. For these and other reasons it seems clear that in meeting its objectives a mature society must be prepared to spend a larger fraction of the national income on education and accept a larger role for government in the financing of these costs.

Medical care is another area in which both public and private expenditures are growing rapidly and in which government is playing an increasingly important role. Private expenditures on medical care as a fraction of total consumer expenditures increased from 4.5 per cent in 1929 to 6.3 per cent in 1960. A high-income society obviously exhibits a high income elasticity of demand for this kind of service. The rate of increase in public expenditures in this area has been even more striking. Furthermore, it is obvious that government will be forced to play a continually larger part. Public opinion in this and in other democratic countries is prepared to tolerate large differences in standards of living as represented by expenditures on housing, food, clothing, recreation, and other objectives. It is much less prepared to tolerate large differences in the standard of medical care. How existing differences can and should be lessened opens up a whole range of questions with which I am not here prepared to cope. There is, however, no doubt in my mind that adequate medical care for all its citizens must be one of the objectives of a mature society and that to attain this objective government will necessarily assume a larger role.

Recreational activities constitute a third area in which expenditures are markedly responsive to high and rising incomes. It is, however, extremely difficult, in the national income statistics, to sort out this type of outlay. Expenditures specifically listed under recreation as a per cent of total consumer expenditures showed only a moderate increase of 5.5 to 5.8 from 1929 to 1960. But this does not include the very large recreational transportation expenditures, the construction of summer houses, and other important segments of this category. If all expenditures properly considered recreational could be included, there is no doubt they would represent a large and rapidly growing fraction of consumer incomes. The manufacture of recreational equipment is, of course, already big business. Private enterprise can not only take care of this but also most of the transportation and construction services connected with recreation. But sporting equipment and transportation facilities are of little use if there is no place to go. The United States has, of course, a magnificent system of national parks and many state park systems, and it behooves us to add to and improve them. But we have lagged woefully behind many other countries in the provision of recreational facilities in the neighborhood of centers of population and in the preservation of existing amenities for public as well as private use.

The pollution of American rivers is an admitted national disgrace. The gobbling-up of seashore and lake-front sites for private use presents shrinking possibilities of public use for rapidly growing urban populations. The only parts of the conservation program that seem to me to have great urgency are the protection of our dwindling water supplies and the enlargement of the natural resource possibilities for public recreational use. These I think must be properly included in any list of objectives for a mature society.

It has been emphasized that a mature high-income society is, among other things, characterized by increasing urbanization, an increasing percentage of the aged in its population distribution, and a shift in consumer demands toward services, particularly toward certain personal and professional services. It has been suggested that these characteristics present problems that will not automatically be taken care of by the maintenance of full employment and persistent growth.

A fourth problem has also been mentioned which involves the choice in an increasingly wealthy economy between work and leisure. Let us postpone for the moment consideration of the last question and look briefly at the implications for public as against private expenditures of the first three.

There can be little doubt that the lion's share of the prospective costs of making our cities fit to live in, of taking care of the increasing percentage of aged in the population, and of meeting the growing demand for education and, to a lesser extent, for recreation will have to come out of the public purse.[5] Is the public purse that capacious and, more particularly, are the revenues flowing to federal, state, and local governments so distributed as to make it possible to satisfy these demands? The United States is already a heavily taxed society. In 1960 the tax revenues accruing to all branches of government amounted to roughly 25 per cent of national income. Furthermore, we lean much more heavily than most European countries on direct taxes, particularly the personal and corporate income tax, and these revenues accrue mainly to the federal government.

So far as our ability to meet the total bill is concerned, the answer depends mainly on our success in attaining full employment and a satisfactory growth rate and on what happens to defense expenditures. The present tax structure and tax rates yield a high marginal return to increases in national income. If we could assume that defense expenditures, which now constitute some three-fourths of the federal outlays, would remain relatively constant in dollars rather than constant as a percentage of the federal budget, the growth in revenues at present tax rates would be amply sufficient to take care of the additional requirements discussed in this paper.

There would, however, even under these relatively favorable circumstances, remain two serious questions. How would these require-

---

[5] This raises the question whether certain functions now carried out by government cannot, in time, be transferred to the private sector. The operation of rural electrical facilities suggests itself as one possibility, and certainly this and other opportunities should be explored. It should be noted, however, that military and war-connected expenditures now account for 85 per cent of federal outlays for goods and services. And so far as state and local expenditures are concerned, their continued increase against strong opposition must represent something like a lower limit of what the community is willing to tolerate in the level of public services.

ments, pressing as they may seem to be, stack up against tax reduction in the competition for public favor? And secondly, would it be possible to bring about a much larger than customary transfer of federal revenues to local use? It is quite clear that the burden of providing the required services is far beyond anything that state and local tax revenues and borrowing capacity can accommodate.

The question of choice between increased expenditures for, say, urban development or care for the aged and tax reduction is a difficult one for a democratic society. There may be substantial support for the proposition that the marginal utility of public expenditures is high, but each individual voter, in comparing the known and particular advantages to him of tax reduction against the general and relatively unknown advantages of an increase in public services, is apt to be strongly biased in favor of the former. There does, however, seem to be a strong asymmetry in public attitudes toward tax reduction as compared to expenditure increases; and political leaders, if they are wise, should take advantage of it. Fiscal history in Western countries appears to show that what is considered to be a tolerable tax burden is largely determined by what the society has become accustomed to. The main upward changes have come about because of wars or serious social disturbances such as the great depression of the 1930's. After a war or a disturbance, tax rates tend not to return to their former level. Burdens that would not be tolerated prewar are rather easily tolerated postwar.[6] This argues strongly for the proposition that we should be slow to reduce tax rates so long as there are recognizably serious and unsatisfied public obligations. We can be sure that once public revenues are reduced it is almost impossibly difficult to raise them for any purpose short of war.

There remains the question of how public revenues, assuming they are large enough to cover high-priority public requirements, can be adequately distributed to the proper expenditure units. Whether this can best be done by increased grants-in-aid, by establishing legal claims on the part of local units to a share in federal revenues, or by an overhaul in the total tax structure favoring state and local units raises too many questions to discuss here. It is obvious, though, that if the objectives of a mature society stressed in this paper are to be attained, some considerable redistribution of expenditures from the federal to the local level will have to be accomplished.

In conclusion, let us take note of the highly speculative question of the choice between work and leisure and how it is likely to be

[6] Cf. the interesting study by Alan T. Peacock and Jack Wiseman, *The Growth of Public Expenditures in the United Kingdom* (Princeton, N.J.: Princeton University Press, 1961).

affected by the increasing per capita incomes of a mature society. The average length of the workweek has, of course, fallen pretty steadily for the last hundred years. Almost all projections of national income over the next quarter-century envisage a continuing decline at something like the rate of the recent past. The observed decline long antedates the emergence of powerful trade unions, and we must assume that in the main it is the product of individual choices between the larger volume of goods and services that would be available with longer hours of work and the disutility that would accompany these longer hours once primary desires are satisfied. What is likely to happen as these primary desires recede into still less importance with rising incomes? Are human desires really insatiable, or will it require a continually larger volume of advertising expenditures to create a demand sufficient to sustain a thirty-five–forty-hour week? According to one thoughtful observer, Herbert Simon, who foresees enormous increases in productivity from automation, "It is hard to believe . . . that man's appetite for gadgets can continue to expand at a rate required to keep work and production in central roles in the society. Even Galbraith's proposal for diverting expenditures from gadgets to social services can only be a temporary expedient. We shall have to, finally, come to grips with the problem of leisure."[7]

If we do have to come to grips with this problem, it seems to me highly important that the choice be in fact between goods and leisure and not between jobs and leisure. The current trade union demand for the thirty-five-hour week is essentially a demand for more jobs and not for more leisure. This pressure is apt to increase so long as the economy operates at substantially less than full employment, and it will become irresistible if unemployment greatly increases. If we do, on the other hand, attain stability and growth, the choice between work and leisure can become what it should be—a social judgment representing individual values freely expressed in the market place.

[7] Herbert Simon, "The Corporation: Will It Be Managed by Machines?" in Melvin Anshen and G. L. Bach (eds.), *Management and Corporations, 1985* (New York: McGraw-Hill Book Co., 1960), p. 54.

SIMON KUZNETS

Notes on the Pattern of U.S. Economic Growth

Economic growth is a long-term process whose features can properly be observed only in a historical perspective. Since its quantitative dimensions, in the aggregate and for major components, are of the essence, its measurement is indispensable. In view of the wide discussion of the country's growth (or lack of growth) during recent years, it may be helpful to take a longer look. Some of the distinctive quantitative characteristics of our economic growth over the long stretch may be useful in evaluating recent changes.

COMPARATIVE LONG-TERM RATES OF GROWTH

Crude as the estimates are, we can approximate the rates of growth of the gross national product, population, and labor force in this country back to 1840—the year that may be accepted as dating the entry of this country into the period of modern industrialization. Over the one hundred and twenty years from 1840 to 1960, population grew at an average rate of about 2 per cent per year; labor force, at a slightly higher rate of 2.2 per cent per year; gross national product, at 3.6 per cent per year; per capita product, at 1.6 per cent per year; and product per worker, at 1.4 per cent per year (Table 1). These rates mean that in 1960 population was about 10.5 times as large as in 1840; labor force, almost 13 times; per capita product and, presumably, per capita real income, over 6 times; and product per worker, over 5 times.

How does this record compare with the long-term growth of other countries? The countries of most interest to us here are those that we now consider developed, i.e., those that have managed to take advantage of the wide potentials of modern economic growth and those that are (or were) fairly large, so that their growth conditions and problems have not been too different from those of the United States.

SIMON KUZNETS is George F. Baker Professor of Economics at Harvard University.

TABLE 1

RATES OF GROWTH PER YEAR, GROSS NATIONAL PRODUCT, POPULATION, AND
LABOR FORCE IN THE UNITED STATES IN SUCCESSIVE AND OVERLAPPING
DECADES AND LONGER PERIODS, 1840–1960 (PER CENT)

	Product* (1)	Population† (2)	Labor Force† (3)	Product per Capita (4)	Product per Worker (5)
Successive decades:					
1. 1839–49	4.24	3.11	3.57	1.10	0.64
2. 1849–59	4.95	3.09	3.18	1.80	1.71
3. 1859–69	1.99	2.39	2.07	−0.39	−0.08
4. 1869–79	4.95	2.33	3.01	2.56	1.88
Overlapping decades:					
5. 1878–82—1888–92	3.73	2.26	2.70	1.44	1.00
6. 1883–87—1893–97	3.10	2.02	2.50	1.05	0.58
7. 1888–92—1898–1902	4.04	1.80	2.50	2.20	1.50
8. 1893–97—1903–07	5.03	1.78	2.60	3.19	2.36
9. 1898–1902—1908–12	3.71	1.95	2.67	1.73	1.01
10. 1903–07—1913–17	2.60	1.87	1.95	0.72	0.63
11. 1908–12—1918–22	2.60	1.50	1.05	1.08	1.53
12. 1913–17—1923–27	3.62	1.40	1.14	2.19	2.45
13. 1918–22—1929	3.99	1.47	1.35	2.49	2.61
14. 1923–27—1933–37	−0.35	0.98	1.16	−1.33	−1.49
15. 1929—1939–41	1.37	0.74	1.21	0.62	0.15
16. 1933–37—1943–47	7.02	0.96	1.84	6.00	5.09
17. 1939–41—1948–52	4.27	1.39	1.40	2.84	2.83
18. 1943–47—1953–57	2.47	1.67	0.80	0.78	1.65
19. 1948–52—1959–61	3.24	1.71	1.19	1.50	2.03
Longer periods:					
20. 1840–80	4.03	2.73	2.96	1.26	1.04
21. 1880–1920	3.52	1.88	2.23	1.61	1.26
22. 1920–60	3.15	1.31	1.28	1.81	1.84
23. 1840–1960	3.56	1.97	2.15	1.56	1.38
Absolute values:‡					
24. 1959–61§	509.0	179.9	69.9	2,829	7,282
25. 1959–61 as multiple of 1840‖	66.7	10.4	12.9	6.4	5.2
26. 1840#	7.63	17.1	5.42	446	1,408

* For 1839–79 we used estimates in 1879 prices of commodity product (value added in agriculture, mining, manufacturing, and construction) by Robert E. Gallman, "Commodity Output, 1839–1899," in *Trends in the American Economy in the Nineteenth Century* ("Studies in Income and Wealth," Vol. XXIV [Princeton, N.J.: Princeton University Press, 1960]), Table 1, p. 16. Since the ratio of these estimates adjusted to 1929 prices for 1874–99 (for each fifth year) to those of gross national product (quinquennial averages centered on the same years) is relatively constant—it fluctuates from 0.58 to 0.67, without any trend—we assumed that the rate of growth of commodity product for 1839–79 represents the rate of growth of gross national product.

For 1878–82—1918–22 the estimates in 1929 prices are from Simon Kuznets, *Capital in the American Economy* (Princeton, N.J.: Princeton University Press, 1961), Table R-26, Variant III, pp. 563–64.

For 1918–22—1959–61 the estimates in 1961 prices are those of the Department of Commerce, given in the *Economic Report of the President* (January, 1962), Table B-2, p. 208. For 1929–58 the estimates have been extrapolated from 1958–61 by gross national product in 1954 prices, given in the *Survey of Current Business* (July, 1962), Table 5, p. 8; and they have been extrapolated from 1929 to 1918 by the 1954 price estimates in U.S. Department of Commerce, *U.S. Income and Output* (Washington, 1958), Table I-16, pp. 138–39, and Table I-2, pp. 118–19.

The estimates for 1960 and 1961 given in the *Survey* were reduced $1 billion to exclude Alaska and Hawaii. This adjustment was indicated for 1960 in the *Survey*, p. 5, and assumed for 1961, since personal income in the two states in 1961 was less than 5 per cent larger than in 1960.

† Before 1880, the values are for the census years, given in the U.S. Bureau of the Census, *Historical Statistics of the United States* (Washington, 1960), Series A-20, p. 8, and Series D-57, p. 74. For 1878–82—1918–22 they are from Simon Kuznets, *op. cit.*, Table R-37, pp. 624–26, and Table R-39, pp. 630–31, and include armed forces overseas. For 1918–22—1959–61 they are those given in the *Economic Report of the President* (January, 1962), Table B-16, p. 227, and Table B-19, p. 230 (including armed forces for 1929–61), and extrapolated to 1918–22 by the Kuznets series on the basis of the relationship in 1933–37. The population figures for 1960 and 1961 were reduced by population of Alaska and Hawaii, given in the U.S. Bureau of the Census, *Population Reports* (Series P-25, No. 258 [November 21, 1962]); and labor force for 1960, excluding the two states, was extrapolated to 1961 by the movement in labor force (including the two states) from 1960 to 1961.

In lines 5–19 the initial and terminal values are arithmetic means of the five- or three-year period shown in the stub, except for 1929, where we used the single year to exclude the years of the thirties. In lines 20–23, the rates are geometric means of those for the underlying successive decades, and those for 1839–79 are assumed to apply to 1840–80.

‡ Product is listed in billions of 1961 dollars; population and labor force, in millions; and product per capita and per worker, in 1961 dollars.

§ Cols. 1 and 2 are the absolute values underlying line 19; col. 3 = line 25 × line 26; col. 4 = col. 1 ÷ col. 2; col. 5 = col. 1 ÷ col. 3.

‖ These figures are based on cumulated growth rates.

Col. 1 = line 24 ÷ line 25; cols. 2 and 3 are the values underlying line 1; col. 4 = col. 1 ÷ col. 2; col. 5 = col. 1 ÷ col. 3.

If then we look at the long-term records of countries like the United Kingdom, France, Germany, Russia (and the U.S.S.R.), and Japan, allow for changes in boundaries, and observe long periods (ranging from seventy-nine years for Japan to one hundred and seventeen years for the United Kingdom), the results of the comparison may be stated simply (Table 2). First, the annual rate of growth of population in the United States was much higher than in these other large, developed countries: compared with 2 per cent in this country, the rates in the other countries ranged from 1.2 per cent for Japan to 0.2 for France and, except for Japan, were half or less than half of the rate of growth of U.S. population. Second, the annual rates of growth of per capita product for the United States and for the large European countries were within a fairly narrow range: from 1.9 per cent for Russia (for a period reaching back to 1860) to 1.2 per cent for the United Kingdom (for a period reaching back to 1841), with 1.5 to 1.6 per cent for this country. We cannot place much stress on such differences, and for practical purposes, we can assume that the U.S. rate of growth in per capita product was about the same as in the large, developed European countries. The Japanese rate, estimated for 1880–1960 at 2.8 per cent, was distinctly higher. Third, the much higher rate of growth of population in the United States, combined with the same or roughly the same rate of growth of per capita product, means that there was a correspondingly higher rate of growth in aggregate product here than in the European countries. Thus, the rate of rise in gross national product in the United States was from a fifth to almost twice as high as that in the large, developed European countries.

It need hardly be mentioned that these averages are for long periods, covering subperiods that differ markedly in the rates of growth of product and population. Furthermore, for several countries, particularly Japan, the period is significantly shorter than that for the United States; and extension of the period to 1840, the initial date for this country, would only lower the averages for both the European countries and for Japan. Yet the comparison is valid and indicates the exceptional performance in the United States: high rates of growth of population and of total product, if not of per capita product, have existed over the long period of the past one hundred and twenty years.

The conclusions just noted would be modified only slightly if we were to extend the comparison to the smaller, developed European countries like Denmark, Norway, Sweden, and the Netherlands—to list the four for which we have long-term records. In general, the rate of growth of population in the United States was much higher

TABLE 2

RATES OF GROWTH PER YEAR, PRODUCT, POPULATION, AND PER CAPITA PRODUCT FOR SELECTED COUNTRIES OVER LONG PERIODS* (PER CENT)

	Duration of Period† (1)	Product (2)	Population (3)	Product per Capita (4)
	Great Britain and United Kingdom‡			
Great Britain:				
1. 1841–81	40	2.54	1.19	1.33
2. 1881–1921	40	1.77	0.91	0.86
United Kingdom:				
3. 1921—1957–59	37	1.88	0.43	1.44
4. Total, 1841—1957–59	117	2.07	0.86	1.20
	France§			
5. 1841–50—1861–70	20	2.23	0.39	1.84
6. 1871–80—1901–10	30	2.00	0.22	1.77
7. 1901–10—1920–28	18.5	1.46	−0.13	1.60
8. 1920–28—1958–60	35	1.55	0.37	1.18
9. Total, 1841–50—1958–60	103.5	1.80	0.24	1.55
	Germany‖			
1913 boundaries:				
10. 1851–55—1871–75	20	1.63	0.74	0.89
11. 1871–75—1913	40	3.09	1.20	1.87
Interwar boundaries:				
12. 1913—1935–37	23	0.57	0.53	0.04
Federal Republic:				
13. 1936—1958–60	23	3.97	1.40	2.53
14. Total, 1913—1958–60	46	2.25	0.97	1.28
15. Total, 1851–55—1958–60	106	2.45	1.01	1.43
	Sweden♯			
16. 1861–65—1881–85	20	2.88	0.72	2.15
17. 1881–85—1921–25	40	2.69	0.66	2.01
18. 1921–25—1958–60	36	3.77	0.59	3.16
19. Total, 1861–65—1958–60	96	3.13	0.64	2.47

* Unless otherwise indicated, all series were brought up to date by use of various issues of the United Nations *Yearbook of National Accounts Statistics* and its *Demographic Yearbook.*

† For series with initial or terminal periods longer than one year, duration is calculated between midyears.

‡ All the estimates are from Phyllis Deane and W. A. Cole, *British Economic Growth, 1688–1959* (Cambridge: Cambridge University Press, 1962). Population for Great Britain for 1841–1921 is from Table 3, p. 8; that for the United Kingdom (in present boundaries) for 1921 and 1958 is derived from Table 90, pp. 329–31. Per capita income for Great Britain for 1841 and 1881, in average 1865 and 1885 prices, is given in Table 72, p. 282; and we estimate it for 1921 by extrapolating from 1901 on the basis of per capita income in 1913–14 prices for the United Kingdom. The latter is given annually in Table 90. We estimated total national income by multiplying population by per capita income.

§ The main series for France are from Simon Kuznets, "Quantitative Aspects of the Economic Growth of Nations: I. Levels and Variability of Rates of Growth," *Economic Development and Cultural Change,* V (October, 1956), Appendix Table 3, pp. 59–60. The estimates exclude Alsace-Lorraine from 1871–80 to 1901–10 and include it from 1841–60 to 1861–70 and 1901–10 to the present. Net national product is in 1938 prices.

‖ The estimates refer to national income in 1913 and 1928 prices and are extrapolated forward by gross national product. The basic sources are: W. G. Hoffmann and J. H. Müller, *Das deutsche Volkseinkommen 1851–1957* (Tübingen: J. C. B. Mohn [Paul Siebeck], 1959), Table 2, p. 14, and Table 14, pp. 39–40 (for 1851–1913); and Paul Jostock, "The Long-Term Growth of National Income in Germany," in Simon Kuznets (ed.), *Income and Wealth* (Series V [Cambridge: Bowes and Bowes, 1955]), Table I, p. 82 (for 1913—1950–52).

♯ Gross domestic product in 1913 prices, 1861–1953, is from Östen Johansson, "Economic Growth and Structure in Sweden, 1861–1953," a mimeographed paper presented at the 1959 meeting of the International Association for Research in Income and Wealth, Table 18, pp. 62–65. The population 1861–1930 is from Erik Lindahl, Einar Dahlgren, and Karin Kock, *National Income of Sweden, 1881–1930* (London: P. S. King & Son, 1937), Part II, Table 64, pp. 4–5.

TABLE 2—*Continued*

	Duration of Period† (1)	Product (2)	Population (3)	Product per Capita (4)
	European Russia and U.S.S.R.**			
European Russia:				
20. 1860–1913...................	53	2.67	1.30	1.35
U.S.S.R.:				
21. 1913–28....................	15	0.54	0.54	0
22. 1928–58....................	30	4.40	0.67	3.71
23. Total, 1913–58..............	45	3.10	0.63	2.45
24. Total, 1860–1958............	98	2.87	0.99	1.86
	Japan††			
25. 1878–82—1918–22...........	40	4.14	1.05	3.05
26. 1918–22—1958–60...........	39	3.97	1.36	2.57
27. Total, 1878–82—1958–60......	79	4.05	1.21	2.81

** For European Russia the basic estimate of commodity product is from Raymond W. Goldsmith, "The Economic Growth of Tsarist Russia, 1860–1913," *Economic Development and Cultural Change,* IX (April, 1961), 471. Population for the pre–World War I period through 1928 is from Frank Lorimer, *The Population of the Soviet Union: History and Prospects* (Geneva: League of Nations, 1946), Table A-2, p. 208 (for 1859 and 1897, European Russia only); Table 15, p. 35 (for 1897 and 1914, prewar European Russia); Table 16, p. 36 and Table 54, p. 135 (for 1914 and 1928, post–World War I Soviet area). We assumed that per capita income in 1928 was the same as in 1913, an assumption supported, for example, by the Birmingham Bureau of Research on Russian Economic Conditions, *The National Income of the U.S.S.R.* (Memorandum No. 3 [November, 1931]), particularly p. 3.

For 1928–58 the product estimates are of national income in 1937 prices, and they and the population figures are from Simon Kuznets, "A Comparative Appraisal," in Abram Bergson and Simon Kuznets (eds.), *Economic Trends in the Soviet Union* (Cambridge, Mass.: Harvard University Press, 1963), Table VIII-2, p. 337.

†† The main source for Japan through the early 1950's is Kazushi Ohkawa *et al., The Growth of the Japanese Economy since 1878* (Tokyo: Kinokuniya Bookstore, 1957), Table 1, p. 7; Table 3, p. 19; Table 2, p. 234. The estimates relate to national income in 1928–32 prices and in 1934–36 prices.

while the rate of growth of per capita product was either about the same or slightly higher or lower—except in comparison with Sweden, which combined a high rate of growth of per capita product, 2.5 per cent, with a low rate of population growth, 0.64 per cent (see Table 2). Indeed, the rapidity of population growth in this country is matched over the long period only in other overseas offshoots of Europe such as Canada, Australia, and Argentina. As a result of this rapid population growth, the United States forged ahead to a position of dominance. In 1840 the population of the United States was about 17 million; that of Great Britain was 18.6 million, significantly larger; those of France and Germany (1913 boundaries) were well over 30 million each, or almost double; and that of Russia was over 50 million, or almost three times as large. In 1960, the population of the United States, 180 million, was over three times as large as that of the United Kingdom, almost four times as large as that of France, two and a half

times the total of East and West Germany, and only about a seventh
below that of the U.S.S.R., despite the recent expansion in the latter's
territory.[1]

One further implication of the conclusions should be noted. We
know that at present the per capita product of the United States is the
highest in the world and appreciably higher than that in the developed
European countries. Such comparisons are treacherous, but this statement is undeniable even if we do not accept at face value the United
Nations estimates that indicate that in 1952–54 per capita income of
the United States was more than double those of the United Kingdom
and France and over three times that of Germany.[2] Nor is it easy to
ascribe meaning to a calculation that shows that per capita product in
the United States was almost three times that of the U.S.S.R. in
1958.[3] But let us assume moderately that the advantage in recent years
is, say, one and one-half to one. Then, if the rate of growth in per
capita income in the United States is about the same as for these
European countries, the implication is that in 1840 the per capita income of the United States was also at least one and one-half times as
high, and relatively higher if the rates of growth of per capita income
in the large European countries were greater than that of the United
States. A crude but suggestive calculation indicates that from the beginning of our period, the per capita income of the United States—
even before its industrialization—was close to that in the most-de-
veloped country, the United Kingdom, and appreciably higher than
in most European countries, let alone the rest of the world (with the
exception of a country like Australia in its very early period of

[1] Population data for other countries for 1840 are from Phyllis Deane and W. A. Cole,
British Economic Growth, 1688–1959 (Cambridge: Cambridge University Press, 1962),
p. 8 (statistics for Great Britain, 1841); and R. R. Kuczynski, *The Balance of Births and
Deaths* (New York: Macmillan Co., 1928), I, 98–99. The estimates for Russia are from
W. S. and E. S. Woytinsky, *World Population and Production: Trends and Outlooks*
(New York: Twentieth Century Fund, 1953), Table 17, p. 44. The estimates for 1960
are from the United Nations, *Demographic Yearbook, 1961* (New York, 1962).

[2] See United Nations, *Per Capita National Product of Fifty-five Countries, 1952–54*
(Statistical Papers, Series E, No. 4 [New York, 1957]).

[3] Abram Bergson (*The Real National Product of Soviet Russia since 1928* [Cam-
bridge, Mass.: Harvard University Press, 1961], p. 261) states that "on the eve of the
five year plans the USSR was producing annually an output on the order of $170
per capita [in terms of 1929 prices]." With such output in 1928 and the rate of growth
in per capita product of 3.71 per cent per year (see Table 2, line 21), per capita product
in the U.S.S.R. in 1958 works out to $507 in 1929 prices, or about $1,020 in 1961 prices,
if we use the ratio of 1961 prices to 1929 prices, 2.01, as given in *Economic Report
of the President* (January, 1962). The U.S.A. gross national product per capita in 1958,
in 1961 prices, is close to $2,680, or over 2.6 times as high.

growth).[4] In other words, the very high per capita income of the United States in comparison to those of other developed countries observed today is due largely to the fact that at the beginning of its industrialization its per capita income was already relatively high, and during the one hundred and twenty years that followed, it managed to sustain rates of growth in per capita income that were not much lower than those of the developed countries that had initially much lower per capita incomes.

CHARACTERISTICS OF LONG-TERM U.S. GROWTH

The high rate of population growth in the United States, higher than in other large, developed countries, was due primarily to the power of this country to attract immigrants. From 1840 to 1930, through three-quarters of the long period covered here, the population of native stock grew from 14.2 to 82.7 million, less than six times the initial number; the population of foreign stock, i.e., foreign-born and native-born of foreign or mixed parentage, grew from somewhat less than 3 million to over 40 million, or over thirteen times the original number; and in 1930, about a third of the country's total popula-

---

[4] Such calculations are necessarily rough and are not fully consistent with comparisons of coterminous estimates in the early years. Thus, from Table 3 and Table 72 of Deane and Cole (*op. cit.,* pp. 8, 282), we can estimate income per capita in Great Britain in 1841 at 24.3, or about $121 at the current rate of exchange. According to Table A-1, Variant A, of Robert E. Gallman, "Commodity Output, 1839–1899," in *Trends in the American Economy in the Nineteenth Century* ("Studies in Income and Wealth," XXIV [Princeton, N.J.: Princeton University Press, 1960]), p. 43, commodity product per capita in 1839 was $60.6 and assuming a ratio of commodity product to national income of 0.65 (it averages about 0.63 of gross national product between 1874 and 1899), we secure a per capita income of $93, which is about a fourth below that of Great Britain. If we apply to the two per capita incomes the rates of growth for one hundred and twenty years, shown in Tables 1 and 2, the ratio of incomes at the end of the period would be 1.18 for the U.S.A. to 1 for Great Britain—an appreciably narrower spread than that between the United States and the United Kingdom as shown by the United Nations figures. While the discrepancy would be reduced by a shift from the per capita income of Great Britain to those of the United Kingdom, most of it would remain. Alternatively, if we estimate gross national product per capita for the United States in 1839 at $96.2 (dividing $60.6 by 0.63) and convert it to 1961 prices by linking the successive price indexes, product per capita for 1839 would be $356 in 1961 prices or, say, $360 for 1840 rather than $446, as shown in Table 1. The discrepancy is due in part to the fact that the Department of Commerce estimate of gross national product in 1918–22, averaging $127.8 billion in 1954 prices and $73.4 billion in 1929 prices, is about 6 per cent larger than the National Bureau of Economic Research estimate of $69.4 billion; this is partly due to the fact that the cumulative rate of growth tends to be reduced by the use of price indexes based toward the end of, or beyond the period of, coverage.

But even allowing for such discrepancies, the rough calculation does suggest orders of magnitude, and it is clear that per capita income in the United States in 1840 was only slightly below that of Great Britain and appreciably higher than those in France and Germany—let alone Russia and Japan.

tion was of foreign stock.[5] Also, the rate of natural increase, i.e., the excess of births over deaths, may have been slightly higher here than in the older, developed countries, with the birth rates higher (particularly in the early nineteenth century) and the death rates somewhat lower. But the major source of the difference in the rate of growth of population and still more in that of the labor force was immigration, in ever-increasing streams and from diverse sources in Europe, although not from other continents. The importance of this stream for the economic growth of the United States is still not fully understood or completely analyzed, much of the past literature having concentrated on difficulties of adjustment and assimilation and having been biased by reformers concerned with short-term problems rather than with long-term gains. Nor have we paid sufficient attention to the effect of the decline in this source of growth in population and labor force—initiated in World War I, furthered by restrictive legislation in the 1920's, and sharply accentuated in the depression of the 1930's, never to be relaxed significantly—on the economic growth and adjustment problems of this country in recent years.

That the rate of growth in per capita product in the United States was no higher than in the large European countries (except moderately, compared with England) and in Japan, despite freedom from destructive impacts of the major wars which affected the latter countries and which are included in the averages cited above, is somewhat of a surprise. As to the comparison with Russia—where the average rate of growth of per capita product was raised largely during the costly three decades under authoritarian rule from 1928 to 1958 and where relative disregard of the more difficult problems of fitting economic growth to the needs and wishes of the population may

[5] The estimates for 1840 are extrapolations of (a) the numbers of foreign-born, first reported in the Census for 1850; (b) the numbers of native-born whites of foreign parentage, first available in 1870; (c) the numbers of native-born whites of mixed parentage, also first available in 1870. For a convenient summary of these data see E. P. Hutchinson, *Immigrants and Their Children, 1850–1950* (New York: John Wiley & Sons, 1956), Tables 1 and 2, pp. 2–3. Foreign-born were derived by subtracting one-half of the cumulated immigration for 1841–50 from the total for 1850; the reduction ratio was derived from comparisons of decennial immigration (given in U.S. Bureau of the Census, *Historical Statistics of the United States* [Series C-88], pp. 56 ff.) with net changes in foreign-born for 1851–60 to 1901–10 (the ratios varied from 31 to 73 per cent). Native whites of foreign parentage were estimated on the basis of the ratio of native whites of foreign parentage, at a given census date, to the average of foreign-born whites at the same and the preceding census dates, the latter being derived by the procedure described above. The ratio, calculated for 1870–1910, ranged from 0.9 to 1.1 The ratio used for the 1840 estimate was 1.0. The native whites of mixed parentage were estimated on the basis of the ratio to native-born whites of foreign parentage, which rose from 0.28 in 1870 to 0.46 in 1910. The ratio used for the 1840 estimate was 0.25. The resulting numbers for 1840 were, in millions: foreign-born—1.38; native whites of foreign parentage—1.23; native whites of mixed parentage—0.31.

account in good part for its high rate of measured economic growth —it is subject to grave doubts, but the results are hardly a puzzle. This is perhaps also true of the comparison with Japan, a country that started from initially very low levels and much later in time and in which a long-lived hierarchical social system was harnessed to the cause of rapid industrialization, while many traditional industries in the fields of consumer goods and housing were preserved. To repeat, the puzzling finding is a rate of growth of per capita product in the United States that was not significantly higher than in France and Germany, only slightly higher than in England, and significantly lower than in Sweden. Could the very rapid rate of growth of population and labor force in this country have made for lower rates of growth in per capita and per worker product than they would have been otherwise? If so, what is the connection? Surely one cannot assume that the supply of natural resources had any limiting effects, insofar as most of the period of growth in the United States is concerned, as compared to the conditions in the European countries. Could the limitation stem from difficulties in supplying adequate capital per worker, engendered by a rapidly growing labor force, despite the high long-term capital-formation proportions in the United States, compared with the other developed countries? Or did the problems of adjustment and assimilation faced by immigrants lower average productivity, despite the fact that most immigrants were in the prime labor ages and presumably endowed with strong economic incentives? Or, finally, did the very high level of per capita income induce a lower rate of growth by permitting the exchange of work for leisure, since there was no great pressure to "catch up"?

These and other questions come easily to mind. But unless the hypotheses underlying them concerning the connection between the high rate of population growth and the less than record rate of growth in per capita or per worker product or between the latter and the high per capita product can be formulated so as to reveal the mechanisms involved, and unless the latter can be studied by means of empirical data, they are not very helpful. Answers to the questions of the type posed require much additional analysis of a variety of long-term data that permit detailed comparison of the United States' rates of growth with those in other countries. This cannot be done in the present paper, and I am compelled to set the questions aside and turn to the examination of other aspects of the long-term rates of growth of product, population, and labor force in the United States. In any case, our observation of these rates should not be limited to averages over as long a period as one hundred and twenty years. How have they changed *during* that period?

First, has there been a long-term acceleration or retardation in the rates of growth? For population and labor force, the answer is clear—the rate of growth has declined markedly. Thus over the first forty years, from 1840 to 1880, despite the fact that the period includes the Civil War years, the population grew 2.7 per cent per year; during the next forty years, the rate dropped to 1.9 per cent per year; in the last forty years, from 1920 to 1960, it was only 1.3 per cent per year. Likewise, the rates of growth in the labor force, through the successive forty-year periods, declined from 3.0 to 2.2 to 1.3 per cent per year. To be sure, population growth has recovered since World War II; the rate of increase over the last decade (1950 to 1960) was 1.7 per cent per year, but it still was lower than the rate for 1880 to 1920; and the rate of growth of the labor force in the last decade was among the lowest, less than 1.2 per cent per year (reflecting the low birth rate of the 1930's), but it may recover to higher levels in the 1960's.

The retardation in the rate of growth of population and labor force was accompanied by a decline in the rate of growth of aggregate gross national product. It was slightly over 4 per cent per year from 1840 to 1880, 3.5 per cent per year from 1880 to 1920, and 3.1 per cent per year from 1920 to 1960 (over the last decade, it was 3.2 per cent per year). It should be noted that except for the earliest period, all product rates are calculated from either five- or three-year averages at terminal points, to reduce the effects of short, cyclical disturbances.

But while the rates of growth of population and labor force declined to less than half of the early levels, the retardation in the rate of growth of gross national product was much less marked—about a quarter. This means, of course, that the rate of growth of per capita or per worker product showed a significant acceleration. The rate of growth of per capita product from 1840 to 1880 was 1.3 per cent per year; from 1880 to 1920 it was 1.6 per cent per year; from 1920 to 1960 it was 1.8 per cent per year; and even in the last decade it was only slightly below 1.6 per cent per year. The per worker product rate was slightly above 1 per cent per year from 1840 to 1880; 1.3 per cent per year from 1880 to 1920; and over 1.8 per cent per year from 1920 to 1960. Over the last decade, from 1950 to 1960, the rate of growth of gross national product per worker was 2.0 per cent per year, among the highest in the long-term record.[6]

[6] A study under way by Professor Gallman, who kindly made some partial results available to me, indicates that the rate of growth of gross national product for 1839–79 may be somewhat higher than that shown in Table 1, with the average rise per year for 1839–59 being of the order of 4.9 per cent rather than the 4.6 shown. If final calculations confirm this preliminary finding and we extend the relative upward adjustment to the full period, the average percentage rise per year in gross national product for 1839–79 would be 4.29, instead of 4.03; in product per capita—1.52, instead of 1.26; in

Two important recent monographs, one for the period since the 1880's and the other for the period since 1909, show acceleration in the rate of growth of product per worker.[7] At the danger of overburdening this paper with statistical detail, I shall give the major conclusions of these studies in a brief listing. The conclusions of the Kendrick study are: (1) Between 1879–1919 and 1919–53, the rate of growth of national product per unit of labor input (man-hours weighted by hourly wage rates in the base year) rose from 1.4 to 1.9 per cent per year; the rate of growth of product per unit of capital input rose from 0.4 to 1.2 per cent per year, and that of product per unit of combined factor input rose from 1.1 to 1.7 per cent per year. (2) The measured acceleration in the rate of growth of productivity was kept down by the inclusion of the government sector and the finance and services sector, for both of which measures of productivity are quite tenuous. When these were excluded, the rise in product per unit of labor input accelerated from 0.8 per cent per year in 1879–1919 to 2.4 per cent in 1919–53. (3) Within the private domestic economy, excluding finance and services, the acceleration in the rate of growth of product per unit of labor input was observed in all sectors except contract construction. (4) Findings for individual sectors and for branches of manufacturing suggest that the divisions of the productive system in which the greatest acceleration in the rate of growth of product per unit of labor (or total factor) input occurred were either those in which such growth was quite low in the past (e.g., agriculture, wood-working manufactures) or those in which technological changes were particularly conspicuous (e.g., chemicals, petroleum, and electrical machinery, among manufactures).

The Denison study also shows a rise in the rate of growth of national product per unit of factor input—from 1.2 per cent per year for 1909–29 to 2 per cent per year for 1929–57 (per man-hour of labor from 1.9 to 2.5). From the analysis that attempts to allocate productivity to the various components, we can gather that of the increase in the rate of growth of productivity of some 0.8 per cent per year (i.e., from 1.2 to 2), greater education of the labor force

product per worker—1.29, instead of 1.04. The broad trends—retardation in the rate of growth of gross national product and acceleration in the rate of growth of product per capita and per worker—would remain largely as now shown. With the same change for 1840–80, the average percentage rises per year for the full period 1840–1960 would be 3.65 for gross national product, instead of 3.56; 1.65 for product per capita, instead of 1.56; and 1.47 for product per worker, instead of 1.38.

[7] See John W. Kendrick, *Productivity Trends in the United States* (Princeton, N.J.: National Bureau of Economic Research, 1961); and Edward F. Denison, *The Sources of Economic Growth in the United States and the Alternatives before Us* (Supplementary Paper No. 13 [New York: Committee for Economic Development, 1962]).

accounts for 0.32 points while of the remainder the major portion is likely to be accounted for by an increased weight credited to the advance of knowledge.[8]

Despite the difficulties of establishing long-term trends in records for the European countries and Japan, affected far more by wars and revolutions than this country, it is clear that no common pattern of marked retardation in the rate of growth of population and total product and of acceleration in the rate of per capita product exists. To be sure, for Great Britain–United Kingdom, the rate of population growth dropped from 1.2 per cent per year in 1841–81 to 0.4 per cent in 1921–58, and in Russia, wars and revolution reduced the rate of population growth from 1.3 per cent per year for 1860–1913 to 0.6 per cent in 1913–58. But in France, Germany, Sweden, and Japan, either there was no marked trend in the rate of population growth, or there was, if anything, an acceleration. And one can infer reasonably that if the rate of population growth did not decline, it is unlikely that the rate of growth of the labor force did. Nor is there much indication of a long-term upward trend, like that observed for the United States, in the rate of growth of per capita product in the European countries and in Japan—except for the effects of the revolutionary break in Russia. England, France, Germany (except for the initial acceleration after 1870), and Japan show no increase in the rate of growth of per capita product and that of Sweden emerges only in the last period, largely since the 1940's.

VARIABILITY OF GROWTH IN THE UNITED STATES

While it is tempting to speculate on the implications of a combination of retardation in the rates of growth of the population and the labor force with acceleration in the rate of growth of product per capita and per worker, a distinctive feature of long-term growth in this country, we must turn now to a third aspect of our experience —the variability of growth. The rates of growth for each decade— calculated wherever possible from five-year averages centered on the initial and terminal years and thus largely eliminating the effects of business cycles of three to nine years in duration—fluctuate widely (Table 1). Even from the 1870's to World War I, a period unaffected

---

[8] With an allowance for the increased education of the labor force of 0.32 and for other sources of increased quality of labor of 0.13, the rate of growth in product per unit of factor input rises from 0.56 in 1909–29 to 0.93 in 1929–57, or 0.37 points (see Denison, *op. cit.*, Table 32, p. 266). Of the 0.56 in 1909–29 and 0.93 in 1929–57, 0.28 and 0.27, respectively, are assigned to economies of scale, which leaves 0.28 and 0.66 as residuals. Of the latter, as much as 0.58 is assigned to advance of knowledge. It is thus defensible to argue that much of the difference between 0.28 and 0.66 must be due to a lower weight for "advance of knowledge" in the earlier period.

by a major war, the rate of growth in per capita product varied between a low of about 1.1 per cent per year (from 1883–87 to 1893–97) to a high of 3.2 per cent per year (from 1893–97 to 1903–7). Swings of approximately twenty years in the growth rates of aggregate product, population, labor force, and product per capita and per worker are observable even after we cancel out as best we can the short-term business cycles.

These long swings in the rate of growth have been the subject of increasing attention in recent years in this country, and the literature dealing with them has grown markedly.[9] Their relevance to the interpretation of recent short-term changes is being examined afresh.[10] Consideration of the technical details of the procedures for the isolation and description of these long swings and of the controversial hypotheses advanced in attempts to account for them would be out of place here. A few general comments may, however, point up the significance of these swings for the present discussion.

First, regardless of the procedure employed to eliminate the short-term business cycles or to distinguish the sustained, unidirectional long-term trends, if we limit the cancellation to cycles that are completed within a decade at most and if we stipulate that the underlying long-term trends make no more than one turn in a period of at least forty to fifty years, the resulting smoothed indexes of product, population, and labor force, as well as the per capita and per worker product, would show significant variations around the underlying long-term trend. And if we describe these variations effectively, their amplitude is found to be significantly wide in relation to the average rate of growth in the underlying trend—to the point where, at the peak of a swing, the decadal rate of growth may be over twice as high as in the underlying trend, and at the trough, less than half as high. It is hardly surprising that even if we disregard periods affected by wars and revolutions and cancel out the short-term cycles, the course

[9] The most convenient summary appears in Moses Abramovitz' statement in the *Hearings on Employment, Growth and Price Levels* (86th Cong., 1st sess. [1959]), Part II, pp. 411–66, and his "The Nature and Significance of Kuznets Cycles," *Economic Development and Cultural Change*, IX (April, 1961), 225–48. See also Simon Kuznets, "Long Swings in the Growth of Population and in Related Economic Variables," *Proceedings of the American Philosophical Society*, VII (February, 1958), 25–37, and his *Capital in the American Economy* (Princeton, N.J.: Princeton University Press, 1961), chaps. 7 and 8, pp. 316–88.

[10] See the following articles in *American Economic Review Papers and Proceedings*, LIII, No. 2 (May, 1963): Bert G. Hickman, "The Postwar Retardation: Another Long Swing in the Rate of Growth?" 490–507; Burnham O. Campbell, "Long Swings in Residential Construction: The Postwar Experience," 508–18; Jeffrey G. Williamson, "Dollar Scarcity and Surplus in Historical Perspective," 519–29; and the discussion of the three papers, 530–40.

of economic performance is not a simple curve that can be adequately and fully described by a second-degree equation over a period of five to fifteen decades. The capacity to attain such a smooth and sustained performance would in itself be more surprising than the observed variability and would require as much explanation as the latter.

Second, granted that the long swings in product may be due in part to prolonged underutilization of economic capacity, we must not overlook the long swings in the rates of growth of population and labor force. So long as the latter are present, even the full utilization of labor and capital will not eliminate the long swings in the rate of growth of aggregate product; and if the swings in population and labor differ in timing, as they well may if they originate in processes of natural increase, there will be long swings also in the rate of growth of output per capita, even under full employment. Thus, in the United States, the rate of population growth reached a low of 0.8 per cent per year in the 1930's, and while this was due to the depression coming on top of the contraction phase of a long swing, it produced a low rate of growth in labor force in the 1950's, about twenty years later. A low growth rate in the labor force leads to a low rate of aggregate growth, even under full employment, unless there is an opposite swing in the rate of growth of product per worker.

Finally, as we would expect, long swings can be found in the rates of growth of other developed economies, these are observable particularly for those for which we have long records of growth.[11] Even in Sweden, a country for which we have tolerably good continuous estimates for a full century, from 1861 to 1960, and one that sustained a high rate of growth in product per capita, the decadal rates of growth in the latter varied from 0.9 and 1.3 per cent per year, on the low side, to 3.7 and over 4 per cent per year on the high side, while the rate of growth in total gross domestic product varied from 1.5 to over 5.5 per cent per year. More than two long swings can be discerned within the one hundred years. And the rates of growth in the Communist countries would probably show the same variability, if there were a long enough record undisturbed by wars or revolutions. The "echo" effects of downward swings in the rates of growth of population and labor force, even if occasioned by wars, are just as marked for the Communist countries; and in addition, the errors in planning and the struggles for political succession and their associated policy choices cannot help but affect rates of growth for periods long enough to constitute phases of long swings.

[11] See a preliminary summary in Simon Kuznets, "Quantitative Aspects of the Economic Growth of Nations: I. Levels and Variability of Rates of Growth," *Economic Development and Cultural Change*, V (October, 1956), 44–51.

Recent Growth in the Context of the Secular Trend

What is the relevance of the findings discussed above to the evaluation of recent growth in this country? To be sure, one may deny any relevance—either because the underlying estimates are judged to be completely unreliable or because it may be argued that the present is separated from the past by a void that prohibits any inference from a long-term perspective. The first argument rests on technical grounds, and all one can say against it is that despite obvious limitations, rough estimates of the longer past are far more useful than more precise data within a short-term span that do not permit comparisons over time. The second argument implies that we are in a completely new era, not only in the sense that conditions are new but that even our inheritance from the past has been dissipated or is irrelevant—an assumption that cannot be accepted because it disregards the many important ways in which the past has shaped this country's observable responses to new problems.

The difficulty is not in a general demonstration that long-term levels, trends, and variability of the rates of growth are relevant to the evaluation of recent growth experience here and abroad, but rather in formulating this evaluation, in establishing the full bearing of the past upon the recent present and the proximate future. And the difficulty stems from the fact that these quantitative findings on the past are relatively new, that we do not know, in an empirically testable fashion, the factors, particularly the institutional adjustments, that were involved in the growth trends and in their long swings— so that even if we could establish the current and prospective conditions under which the economy would be operating, we have no fully learned lesson of the past to apply to them. The speculations suggested above on the relation between our high rate of growth of population and labor force and our not-so-high rate of growth in product per capita and per worker, similar questions concerning the association between the marked retardation in the rates of growth of our population and labor force and the significant acceleration in the rate of growth of per capita and per worker product, and our inadequate knowledge of the mechanism that produces the long swings —all point to the meagerness of analytical understanding of these basic quantitative aspects of the country's economic growth, which are so directly relevant to the evaluation of our recent or prospective growth rates.

The above may well be an overstatement, for it disregards the significant contribution to our understanding of aggregative growth which is made by the consideration of structural and international aspects—neither of which we did, or could, treat here except by incidental reference. If, in addition to dwelling on the average level, the retardation or acceleration, and the long swings in the rates of aggregate growth, we could deal also with the associated changes in the industrial structure of the product and the labor force, in the distribution of incomes between those from labor and those from assets or by size of income among various groups in the population, in the allocation of total output between consumption and capital formation, in the share of the country's output per capita linked with others by foreign trade or capital flows, the significance of long-term trends in these aspects of economic growth on the evaluation of current changes and problems would appear far greater and more directly illuminating than our limited discussion of the aggregative measures suggests; and our knowledge would not seem so limited. But we can only remind ourselves of these structural and international aspects of economic growth, without being able to deal here with the pattern of their long-term changes.

Under the circumstances, we can only raise a few questions about the evaluation of recent changes, but even these are worthwhile if they expose the danger of easy judgments and too ready answers. The first and most obvious question is in regard to the meaning of the term "growth" when it is applied to changes over short periods—and they have to be short when we deal with current policy problems. If we say that from 1955 to 1960, the United States' gross national product grew x per cent per year, and we are concerned over the low rate observed, does growth, whether of total or of per capita gross national product, mean the underlying trend *plus* the long swing around it? If so, how can we distinguish the underlying trend? How can we distinguish the factors that affect our long-term growth from those that cause the long swings and further distinguish these from the factors associated with deviations from full employment in the business cycle—so that in choosing policy actions directed at the short-term movements we do not neglect the possible effects on the rate of growth in the underlying long-term trend?

Whatever the answer to this question, and its vital importance is obvious, one clear implication of our earlier discussion is the need not only for a sharp distinction between the shorter and the longer periods when measuring the rate of economic growth but also for care in comparing these rates. The relevance of this comment can be illustrated by a citation from the January, 1962, *Economic Report of the President*. Table 11 of the report contains rates of growth of gross national product per man-year for eleven countries, the United States among them, for the periods 1913–59 and 1950–59. For all the countries the rates are substantially higher for 1950–59 than for 1913–59. The accompanying text reads: "Further evidence that modern industrial economies are not helpless prisoners of past long-term trends is to be found in Table 11, which shows that the major countries of Western Europe, and Japan as well, have recently exceeded their own long-term performance" (p. 114). This statement may have been intended merely to argue against a naïve acceptance of statistically established long-term trends as true descriptions of the paths that economies had to follow and as the bases for projections into the future. But the statement can also be easily read as suggesting that the 1950–59 rates of change constitute a new long-term trend. Yet comparisons between rates of growth for a nine- and a forty-six-year period do not tell us that the long-term trend in the specific nine-year period was different from that in the forty-six-year period; there may have been other nine-year periods that, as phases of long swings, also greatly exceeded the average trend rate for the long period of half a century, and clearly the short-term elements in a nine-year period must be examined for their effect on the average for that period as a measure of long-term trend.[12] Since at least eight of the eleven countries cited in the table were adversely affected by World War II, since the subsequent recovery processes have lasted through most of 1950–59, and also since the four countries with the highest rates of growth for 1950–59—Japan, Italy, Germany, and France—were among those most damaged by the war, such an interpretation of the differences between the rates of growth for the recent nine years and for the longer period of forty-six years would seem incautious.

Second, care must also be exercised in comparing rates of growth for short periods among countries—for they may not portray even roughly the differentials in the underlying long-term trends. In the table in the *Economic Report of the President*, already referred to, the United States, whose rate of growth in gross national product per man-year in 1950–59 was 2.2 per cent per year, is eighth in rank, with six European countries and Japan all showing appreciably higher rates for the same nine-year period. But if, from the same table, we calculate the rates of growth for 1913–50, the preceding thirty-seven years, the rate of growth for the United States, 1.7 per cent per year, is only slightly below that for Japan, 1.8 per cent, and much above the rates for all the other nine countries, particularly the large Euro-

[12] In the original paper that contained the table discussed in the *Economic Report of the President* (January, 1962), the authors' note that "these rapid rates [i.e., the ones for 1950–59] are not unprecedented" and refer to past periods of growth at rates as fast. See Deborah C. Paige, *et al.*, "Economic Growth: The Last Hundred Years," reprinted in Edmund C. Phelps (ed.), *The Goal of Economic Growth* (New York: W. W. Norton & Co., 1962), pp. 69–87, especially p. 86.

pean countries. One is tempted to argue, in line with the suggestion already made, that the high rates of growth in Europe and Japan in recent years have been due in large part to attempts to "catch up" in two ways: first, to recover from the war and, second, to take advantage of the opportunities for greater growth in productivity that were previously utilized in the United States and not, for various reasons, in these other countries. This does not deny the possibility that the acceleration in the rate of economic growth in Europe contains elements—partly associated with the Common Market and partly caused by a shift in public policy—that may induce persistently higher rates of growth than were attained in the long-term pre–World War II past. But it would require discriminating analysis to establish these secular elements making for high growth, and no easy inferences can be drawn from simple statistical comparisons for recent short periods.

FUTURE GROWTH AND INHERITED INSTITUTIONS

The comments above should not be taken to mean that we need not concern ourselves with short-term changes in the level of the country's performance or that we can trust that even if they indicate a lag, the underlying secular trend will somehow eventually sweep us onward to higher levels. If rates of increase in the country's performance slow down, if persistent unemployment of labor and other resources develops, policy action must be considered—whether or not it has been attempted in the past—for we are continuously expanding our knowledge of methods of stimulating and sustaining an economy's growth. But this granted, the value of relating these short-term changes to the longer run of the economy is undeniable, and it would be enhanced if the application of the longer perspective were based on better knowledge and understanding of our past. Consider, for example, the finding that in the last forty years the rate of growth of product per capita and per worker in this country was distinctly higher than in the past—and this despite the inclusion of the period of the 1930's, with the greatest depression on record. Was this merely the result of the retardation in the rate of growth of population and labor force? Should we consider an entirely different hypothesis, one which would assume that the course of technological change since the late nineteenth century permitted increasing rates of growth of product per worker or even per man-hour and that this country was able to exploit this potential, unlike the countries in Europe, which suffered devastating wars and faced other obstacles (overcome only recently)? Conversely, how much of the higher rate of growth of product per capita or per worker in recent decades in this country has been associated with World War II and its aftermath? The implications of these different questions, in terms of the different groups of factors that would have to be examined, are obvious enough; and depending upon the answers, different interpretations of the recent past and proximate future would be suggested, and different policies would seem relevant.[13]

It is tempting to conclude this paper with one rather general comment on the implications of our long-term pattern of economic growth. This growth occurred through decades marked by a succession of turbulent changes in this country and in the rest of the world, and these changes have been particularly rapid since World War I, i.e., in the last third of the long period covered by Table 1. From a relatively small and young country, protected by what were then wide ocean distances as well as the *Pax Britannica*, open to immigration from the more advanced countries of the time, i.e., those in Europe, the United States has emerged to a position of leadership, of dominant size and high level of per capita and per worker economic performance, but vulnerable and exposed to all the dangers of leadership in a divided world in which technological advance means not only gains in peaceful productivity but also more extreme gains in destructiveness of weapons. And much of the change in the international scene was concentrated in the brief span of thirty years, from the 1930's to date.

These trite observations are made to suggest what may not be so obvious—that the pattern of past growth leaves its impression in the institutions that the country develops to deal with the problems generated by past growth; that these institutions may persist beyond their

[13] After having observed the acceleration in the rate of growth of productivity in the United States, characterized as a "break in the trend," John W. Kendrick comments briefly as follows:

"It is not possible adequately to analyze the factors that may have been responsible for the change in productivity trend around the time of World War I. . . . A step in this direction can be taken by noting a few changes that occurred about the same time in associated variables. The scientific management movement, based on the ideas of Frederick W. Taylor, spread widely in the 1920's; college and graduate work in business administration expanded rapidly; and it was only after 1919 that organized research and development became a significant feature of the industrial landscape. . . . It has also been suggested [by Professor Milton Friedman] that the drastic change in national immigration policy promoted a more rapid increase in the average education of the labor force. That is, since the immigrants had less schooling, on the average, than the domestic labor force, the mass influx of workers from abroad prior to World War I had tended to retard the increase in average education.

"It is tempting to enumerate specific innovations that became important after 1919, such as mass or 'flow' production techniques in manufacturing. Certainly, there was a remarkable acceleration in manufacturing productivity in the 1920's. But significant innovations were occurring throughout the whole period; short of a thorough study of their cost-reducing impact, it would not be possible to isolate those that contributed most to the speeding-up of productivity advance" (*op. cit.*, pp. 70–71).

useful time and constitute obstacles to further growth under changed conditions; and that sustained economic growth requires continuous adjustments of social and political institutions to changed conditions— adjustments that are in good part required because the institutions that proved useful earlier and were, in fact, required in earlier economic growth are now obsolete. The impressive record of economic growth in this country was not accomplished by the repetitive application of invariant rules of economic and social behavior; it had to be a creative adjustment to changed conditions, and the cost of some of the conflicts that had developed between old and new institutions (the most striking and costly example was the Civil War) was quite high. Minimization of such costs of adjustment is as desirable today as it ever was, and the general point that economic growth almost naturally produces obsolescence and thus requires attention and drive to remove the resulting obstacles could, I believe, be illustrated today.

The following illustrations are, unfortunately, *ad hoc* examples rather than the results of thorough study. The whole system of primary and, to some extent, even secondary education in this country in the past has played a profound socializing role—as an institution for the assimilation, if not so much of the foreign-born immigrants themselves, of their children. Without it, the unity and consensus so important in making the social decisions necessary to resolve possible conflicts (many of them originating from growth) would not have been secured. Yet, despite the pressure developing for higher educational standards and more advanced levels throughout the system, the tradition of the schools as a way of life rather than a way of learning is not easily overcome. And again speculating on the influx of immigrants and the increasing proportion of foreign stock in this country, one wonders whether some of the distinctive aspects of political organization in the United States have not been, in part, a consequence. Could the resistance to reapportionment of voting power, in response to greater growth of urban population, be rationalized, in part, as an attempt to limit the political power of groups among whom the foreign-born and those of foreign stock are far more predominant than in the non-urban areas, and was the attainment of equality in political power by immigrants and their children delayed much beyond the attainment of economic gains and assimilation? If so, whatever elements of strength and stability were lent to the political system by such past attitudes may have been succeeded by a much more obstructive role of political traditions in dealing with current problems generated by economic growth. And, finally, one may ask whether the emphasis on limitation of federal power and on advantages of decentralized political authority, which in the past fostered so many centers of vigorous economic growth across the country, is equally valid today, when the graver problems of the international scene tend to convert economic growth into a competition rather than permit it to remain a self-determining and self-pacing process.

Perhaps the examples cited above are of dubious validity or, less likely, of small weight. But if at all pertinent, they illustrate the general point urged here—that past patterns of long-term growth leave an economic and institutional heritage which may in part be an obstacle to future growth. If so, understanding past experience may not only mean being able to evaluate properly the significance and likely persistence of current short-term changes in the level of the economy's performance. It may also help to identify those institutional obstacles to further growth that have resulted from adaptation to past growth problems. Likewise, a proper analysis of long-term trends in other countries that are sufficiently similar in organization and orientation for comparison (perhaps with some adjustments), should reveal a variety of growth experience and of feasible institutional changes which may be borrowed with some assurance of their tested contribution. Such understanding of the historical origin and of the obsolescence of institutional arrangements is no guarantee that they can, and will be, effectively modified. But one may hope that knowledge of this type contributes to general social intelligence and should at least weaken the traditional reactions that tend to sanctify, because of long usage, patterns that may have become impediments to possible growth under changed historical conditions.

LESTER V. CHANDLER

Economic Stability

In FEBRUARY, 1946, Congress enacted a law that was to be a land-mark in the history of American economic policy—the Employment Act of 1946. That this was one of the first major pieces of legislation after World War II was no coincidence; it symbolized the high prior-ity of economic stability as a goal of our society. How highly Ameri-cans prized economic stability at that time can hardly be appreciated by those who have not experienced economic instability in its most extreme and painful forms. Memories of the great depression were then still vivid, and fears of its resumption widespread.

Economic instability had, of course, been a matter of concern long before the fateful 1930's. We have had cyclical fluctuations, with alternating periods of prosperity and depression, almost from the beginning of our industrialization. Many had come to believe that such instability is an almost inevitable characteristic of our free-enterprise system, which relies largely on free markets to organize and direct its economic activities and on large numbers of private business firms to employ its resources and produce its output. The achievements of the free-enterprise system have been great indeed. Offering freedom of choice of occupation, freedom to establish and operate enterprises, and freedom of scope for ability and ambition, it is consistent with our general desire for freedom. Under this system we have developed the most productive economy the world has ever seen and achieved the world's highest living standards. Yet none can deny that this performance has been marred by recurring periods of recession and depression, with their huge waste of productive power and their severe hardships for the unemployed and others.

Though the great depression was not our first, it was certainly our worst. Beginning in 1929, it dragged on for a dozen years until it was finally ended by our accelerating rearmament program. At the bot-

LESTER V. CHANDLER is Gordon S. Rentschler Professor of Economics at Princeton University.

tom of the depression in 1932 and 1933, when our total labor force included only about 51 million persons, the number of unemployed averaged over 12 millions. Of those in the labor force nearly one out of four was unemployed. Even after the upturn the situation remained serious. From 1933 until 1941 there was no year in which the number of unemployed fell as low as 7 millions or the percentage of unemployed fell as low as 14 per cent. For the last half of the thirties unemployment averaged 8.5 millions, or more than 16 per cent of the labor force.

If we wished to deal with the matter statistically, we could put dollar values on the huge amounts of output that could have been produced but were not—on the consumer goods that were not turned out and on the factories, equipment, homes, hospitals, schools, and churches that were not built. But there is no satisfactory way of measuring the accompanying hardships and frustrations—the plight of the unemployed who lost both income and status and of those who lost their homes, farms, and savings. Amidst such frustrations, economic, political, and social conflicts became embittered and sharpened. In some other countries facing similar situations, millions seeking economic security turned to totalitarians of the left or right, even at the cost of their liberties. Similar dangers were not absent here. And most tragic of all, the frustrations and conflicts generated by the great depression played an important, and perhaps a vital, role in bringing on World War II.

Such were the roots of the full-employment bill which was introduced in both houses of the Congress at the beginning of 1945, some months before VE Day. It grew out of the extreme economic instability of the 1930's and reflected widespread fears that similar conditions would reappear at the end of the war as government expenditures fell from their wartime peak, orders for munitions and military supplies were canceled, and millions of men and women were mustered out of the armed forces.

The Employment Act of 1946, which gained the unanimous approval of the Senate and passed the House with an overwhelming majority, ranks as a landmark in the history of American economic policy, primarily as a symbol of our aspirations and of the new responsibilities of government for promoting economic stability at high levels of employment. Now a large majority of both Democrats and Republicans of both liberal and conservative persuasion joined in stating that "the Congress hereby declares that it is the continuing policy and responsibility of the Federal government to use all practicable means . . . to promote conditions under which there will be afforded useful employment for those able, willing, and seeking to work, and to promote maximum employment, production and purchasing power."

But however important the Employment Act was as a general statement of policy and responsibility, it certainly was not a blueprint for action. In the process of getting a bill that would be acceptable to all factions, Congress retreated into broad generalities and provided neither the specific definition of goals nor the specific methods of implementation that are required for policy actions. The Act did not even define clearly its employment goals. It was recognized then, as it is today, that various types of frictions and immobilities in labor markets make it impossible to achieve and maintain "full employment" in the literal sense of zero unemployment. But there were then, as now, wide differences of opinion as to how ambitious the goal should be. Some insisted that we should strive for a situation in which the number of job vacancies would always exceed the number of unemployed. Others insisted on less ambitious goals. The Act, by using the general term "maximum employment," left this issue undecided.

The Act provided even less guidance on another set of issues that have in practice presented equally thorny problems—the relationship of employment goals to our other objectives of national policy. It did recognize that such problems would arise, for it stated that the government's actions to promote maximum employment should be "consistent with its needs and obligations and other essential considerations of national policy." Yet it did not even identify these "needs, obligations and other essential considerations"; it did not indicate how they should be ranked relative to employment goals; and it was silent as to what should be done if other considerations came into at least apparent conflict with the promotion of employment objectives.

The Act was no more specific as to the methods to be used to promote its objectives. It did provide for the creation of two new agencies—the Council of Economic Advisers in the Executive Office of the President and the Joint Economic Committee of the Congress. These agencies received power only to study, report, and recommend; power to act remained with the Congress and the Executive Office. The Act did not specify the particular instruments to be used, to say nothing of the relative roles that they should play. However, a study of the legislative history of the Act brings out clearly at least three points of general agreement. First, the purpose was not to supersede or weaken our predominantly free-enterprise system, but rather to strengthen it and improve its stability. In the words of the Act, its objectives were to be promoted "in a manner calculated to foster and promote free competitive enterprise and the general welfare." Second, there was to be a minimum reliance on direct, detailed controls over the policies and actions of consumers and business firms. Few indeed would have voted for the Act if it had contemplated continuing far into the peacetime period the wartime types of controls over prices, wages, allocations, and production. Third, it was generally agreed that the objectives of the Act were to be promoted predominantly through regulation of the aggregate demand for output—the rate of total spending for consumption, investment, and government purposes. This prescription followed from diagnosis of the proximate cause of instability in the past—the instability and self-reinforcing fluctuations of total demand for output. For example, the widespread unemployment and waste of other resources in the 1930's did not reflect any lack of desire on the part of businessmen to hire workers and produce. Rather, it reflected the gross inadequacy of aggregate demand for output—levels of demand so low that business could not find a market for its capacity output at prices high enough to cover costs, to say nothing of yielding profits. The appropriate remedy, therefore, was to achieve and maintain aggregate demand for output at levels which would at all times make it profitable for business to provide maximum employment and production. Many, including business leaders, pointed out that this was essentially a conservative policy. The government's role could be largely limited to that of maintaining aggregate demand at such levels as to induce business to make its maximum contribution to the general economic welfare, and this would not involve direct or detailed government intervention in the market processes determining prices, wages, and production.

What specific instruments should be used to maintain aggregate demand at appropriate levels? Here again the Employment Act itself provides no answer. However, both its legislative history and the thinking of the times indicate primary reliance on two sets of instruments—monetary policy and the government's fiscal policy. To this end, the Federal Reserve System was to use its instruments of general monetary and credit management—its discount policy, open market operations, and control over the legal reserve requirements of banks. If aggregate demand became, or threatened to become, inadequate, the Federal Reserve should increase the supply of money and credit and lower interest rates, thereby stimulating investment spending, which would indirectly stimulate consumption spending as well. If, on the other hand, aggregate demand became so great as to induce price inflation, the Federal Reserve should seek to curb it by restricting the supply of money and credit and raising interest rates.

The general principle that the Federal Reserve should use its monetary policy to promote economic stability is not very controversial, though there is no lack of controversy over the specific policies to be followed. Monetary management has long been a function of the government and the central bank, and most agree that it can be useful. Yet in the postwar period there has been widespread doubt that monetary policy alone can assure the maintenance of appropriate levels of aggregate demand. From the experience of the 1930's, many concluded that monetary policy used alone is incapable of restoring prosperity. My own opinion is that they go too far when they conclude that the episode of the 1930's proves that monetary policy is incapable of bringing recovery. Instead, I would conclude that expansionary policies were so long delayed and so weak that we have no way of knowing how effective a timely and aggressive expansionary monetary policy might have been. Yet I would insist that there are indeed depressed situations in which monetary policy alone will be insufficient to bring full recovery and still more situations in which other measures alone or in conjunction with monetary policy will bring recovery sooner and with less undesirable side effects. There is, indeed, an important and even essential role for fiscal policies.

By the government's fiscal policy we mean, of course, its policies relative to its taxes and expenditures; we shall not discuss here related policies concerning government lending, loan insurance, and debt management. The government obviously must have fiscal policies of some sort, and with government taxing and spending equal to about a quarter of our gross national product these policies inevitably exert an important influence, whether favorable or unfavorable, on aggregate demand for output. The achievement and maintenance of maximum employment and production require that these powers be used to promote an appropriate behavior of aggregate demand. I shall not review here the details of the theory of stabilizing fiscal policy. However, the general principles are relatively simple. The government can support or increase aggregate demand by cutting taxes or by increasing its rate of expenditures. By decreasing taxes, it leaves a larger part of the national income in the hands of families and business firms and enables them to spend more for output. As those enjoying the tax cut spend more, they create more income for others and enable them to demand more output. An increase in government expenditures for output both increases directly the demand for output and creates income for those who supply the government, thereby enabling them to spend more and create more income for others. The government may also increase its expenditures in the form of transfer payments—in such forms as unemployment benefits and relief payments. An increase in government expenditures of these types enables the recipients to spend more, thereby creating more income for others and enhancing their demand for output. Note that in all these cases the total increase in the aggregate demand for output may be expected to be much larger than the initial tax reduction or the initial rise in government expenditures.

Similarly, the government may restrict a rise in aggregate demand for output or actually reduce that demand by raising taxes or by decreasing its rate of expenditures. Here again, the total restrictive effect on aggregate demand may be expected to be considerably larger than the initial rise of taxes or the initial decrease in government expenditures.

It should be clear that the deliberate use of fiscal policy to maintain aggregate demand at levels which will induce maximum employment will frequently, if not usually, be inconsistent with the maintenance of an annually balanced budget or the maintenance of any other fixed relationship between the government's total revenues and total expenditures. Consider first the case of a business recession with falling incomes and rising unemployment. The very decline of national income will reduce the size of tax bases, reduce total tax yields, and tend to turn a budget surplus into a deficit or a deficit into a larger deficit. Yet this is the type of period in which a stabilizing type of fiscal policy calls for tax reduction or an increase of government expenditures. Consider next the case in which aggregate demand is rising to inflationary levels. The very rise of national money income increases the size of tax bases and total tax yields and tends to turn budget deficits into surpluses or to enlarge surpluses. Yet the appropriate fiscal policy for stabilization purposes at such times is likely to call for an increase in effective tax rates or a reduction in government expenditures.

In short, fiscal policy will in case after case be successful in maintaining aggregate demand at appropriate levels only by destabilizing the relationship between the government's total revenues and total expenditures. We shall see later that this type of fiscal policy has run into strong controversy and opposition, that this opposition has decreased both the frequency and aggressiveness of its use, and that this in turn has militated against the success of our program to promote continuous economic stability.

We find, then, that the Employment Act, despite its importance as a statement of intention and of national responsibility, did not provide a blueprint for action, for it did not define in operational terms either its objectives or its methods of implementation. These problems were left to be worked out later. We are still trying to solve these problems and cannot truthfully say that we have found fully satisfactory solutions. The results to date may be called a qualified success. With World War II now more than seventeen years behind us, we have not yet experienced a serious depression like that of the 1930's or even one like that following World War I. The percentage of the labor force unemployed has at no time exceeded 7.5 per cent, and in no year has it averaged above 7 per cent. This represents a real improvement over the performance of the economy in the prewar period, and this has not, I believe, been accidental. Yet the record has been far from perfect. In this postwar period we have had four recessions—those of 1949–50, 1953–54, 1957–58, and 1960–61. Moreover, the last two recoveries have been quite weak, with unemployment remaining considerably above the minimum levels reached in earlier prosperity periods and also well above the minimum unemployment necessitated by imperfections and immobilities in labor markets. It has now been five years since unemployment was as low as 5 per cent, and during most of the time unemployment has been well above this level. There are ominous signs that the maintenance of high levels of employment and output may present even more difficult and challenging problems in the future.

I want to deal now with some of the major problems that have been encountered and that may continue to bedevil us as we seek to promote maximum employment and production. The first set of problems relates to the general topic of this series of lectures: the multiplicity of the nation's economic objectives. And, one should also add, the multiplicity of its political and social objectives.

At the end of World War II, when memories of the great depression were still painfully vivid, many would have said that the objective of promoting maximum employment and production should take precedence over all others. But we know now that we also want many other things involving the economy. We want economic freedom for consumers, workers, and businessmen; stability of price levels; rapid economic growth; a large foreign-aid program for both humanitarian and national security reasons; a large program for national defense; an equitable distribution of income; equilibrium in our balance of international payments; and so on. The list could be extended almost indefinitely.

It would be too pessimistic to conclude that these numerous objectives must inevitably come into conflict with each other and that to promote any one we must sacrifice some of the others. Yet it is clear that where objectives are so numerous, the probability of conflict is increased, and it becomes likely that no one of them will be promoted to the utmost.

Let us look at some relationships among four of these objectives: the promotion of maximum employment, promotion of the rate of economic growth, maintenance of stability of price levels, and promotion of equilibrium in our balance of international payments.

The Employment Act does not mention explicitly the objective of promoting economic growth. Nor could the framers of that Act foresee the unprecedented importance that would come to be attached to this objective in the postwar world. Never before have so many countries been so conscious of the possibility of economic growth or so determined to use national policies to promote it. In the United States we want a higher rate of economic growth for many reasons: to provide more employment oppotrunities; to raise our standards of living; to support on a larger scale our national security program, including foreign aid; and to symbolize the superiority of our economic and social system over that of the Iron Curtain countries. This last objective has received increasing attention as our growth rate has come to lag behind that of many other countries.

Some economists would argue that though the Employment Act did not mention economic growth explicitly, this objective is implicitly included in that of promoting maximum employment, production, and purchasing power. There is much validity in this view. It is clear that the economic stability we seek is not stability on a horizontal or stagnant level. Rather, it is stability on our growth-possibility curve. We can have maximum employment in the sense of minimum unemployment only if actual output rises with our total productive capacity. Unemployment will grow if actual output fails to rise as much as is made possible by the growth of our labor force and of productivity per man-hour. To this degree the objective of promoting economic growth is included in that of promoting maximum employment.

Nevertheless, I contend that the emergent postwar emphasis on economic growth gave at least a new emphasis and even a new dimension to our economic objectives. It seemed to provide an almost independent reason for increasing aggregate demand fast enough to elicit maximum production. It directed attention not only to the rate of total output but also to the composition of output, with a new emphasis on those types of output which would increase productive capacity. If maximum employment were our only objective, we might achieve it with an output composed largely of consumer goods and with little capital formation. The growth objective placed a new emphasis on capital formation. It also became a strong force against the adoption of restrictive monetary and fiscal policies which would be useful in curbing inflation but might inhibit growth. For example, it was cited in opposition to restrictive monetary policies which would raise interest rates and make investment more expensive and against tax policies that might reduce abilities or incentives to save, invest, take risks, or promote technological innovation.

This brings us to another type of economic stability—stability of price levels, or of the purchasing power of the dollar. The Employment Act made no mention of price levels, and repeated proposals that the Act be amended to include price-level stability as an explicit objective of national policy have all failed of adoption. But the fact that this objective is not stated in any law does not mean that it has been an unimportant consideration in national policy. On many occasions the actions of the Federal Reserve and the fiscal authorities have been strongly influenced by their desire to reduce the pace of price increases, if not to achieve complete stability of price levels. Their actions have been more restrictive and less liberal than would have been dictated by considerations relating to employment and growth.

Public and official concern for price-level stability has been greatly enhanced by the large rise of prices during the past two decades. Since 1941 the consumer price index has doubled; the dollar has lost half of its purchasing power over consumer goods. It is important to note, however, that only a small fraction of this increase in the price level can be attributed to peacetime policies of promoting employment and growth. Most of it resulted from World War II and the Korean conflict. Two-thirds of the total price increase since 1941 had occurred by August, 1948, when the wartime and postwar surge of prices had reached its peak. Another one-tenth of it occurred in the ten months following the outbreak in Korea in June, 1950. Only a quarter of it has occurred since March, 1951. Thus in the twelve and a half years since March, 1951, consumer prices have risen only about 18 per cent, or less than 1.5 per cent a year. Such a rate of price increase is hardly frightening in itself and would not have created so much public protest and official concern if it had not been superimposed on the large increases growing out of World War II and the Korean conflict.

Nevertheless, the price increases of the past decade or so have posed serious problems for our policies of promoting maximum employment and growth, primarily because they have so often occurred while unemployment was still considerably above the minimum levels necessitated by frictions and immobilities in labor markets. It had, of course, been recognized that an excessive growth of the aggregate demand for output could create a "demand-pull" inflation of money wage rates and prices. But it had been hoped and expected that this would occur only after unemployment had approached its irreducible minimum and that up to that point increases in aggregate demand would induce an increase in the supply of real output, rather than increases in wages and prices.

Now it appeared that these expectations were too optimistic. We even began to hear that we were experiencing a new type of inflation —not "demand-pull," but "wage-push," "cost-push," "sellers' inflation," or "markup inflation." The general idea was that we had become victims of the monopoly power of big unions and big business— that even in the midst of substantial unemployment the unions demand wage increases in excess of average increases in productivity per man-hour, this raises costs, and business marks up prices. A few economists have even gone so far as to argue that this wage-push, markup process of price inflation is largely independent of the levels of aggregate demand and unemployment and cannot be halted by restricting aggregate demand. Surely this is going too far; surely there is some level of aggregate demand and unemployment that will stop the process. But this is little consolation to a nation desiring both price stability and maximum employment, for the level of unemployment required for price stability may well be excessive in view of our employment and growth objectives.

Thus by the time the prosperity of 1955–57 gave way to the recession of 1958, we were engaged in a serious national debate concerning our objectives relative to employment, growth, and price levels. And there was a growing opinion that these objectives could be reconciled satisfactorily only if we could somehow improve the market processes which determined wages and prices. This debate is not yet ended. But in the meantime, since the end of 1959, the problem has been made much more complex by the intrusion of a new set of considerations—considerations relating to the defict in our balance of international payments and the shrinkage of our net international reserves. Now, for the first time in over thirty years, our freedom to pursue expansionary monetary and fiscal policies to promote employment and growth is jeopardized by the state of our international payments and reserves.

The deficit in our balance of payments did not originate suddenly and dramatically in 1960. Rather, it started as early as 1950. The general pattern during the period has been something like this. Our exports of goods and services have exceeded our imports almost every year, usually by considerable amounts. But our foreign investment and grants to other countries have exceeded our net export balance, and we have paid the difference by giving them gold and short-term claims against dollars. In both ways we have increased the international reserves of other countries. Until about 1960 this process was, on the whole, beneficial to the world and without immediate threat to the international position of the dollar. The continued deficit in the U.S. balance of payments, which continuously increased the gold and dollar reserves of other countries, played a major role in enabling those countries to remove restrictions on international trade and payments and to reconstruct world trade on a liberal basis. At the same time, our gold reserves still seemed large enough to maintain confidence that the United States could meet all its international payments without reducing the value of the dollar in exchange markets and to do this without restricting our freedom to pursue domestic objectives.

In 1960, as the deficit in our balance of payments continued and our net international reserve position continued to deteriorate, the situation changed markedly. For the first time in more than a generation, fears arose that the United States would not be able to redeem in gold all of its short-term dollar liabilities to foreigners and that the dollar might depreciate in exchange markets. These fears were dramatized by large speculative increases in the dollar price of gold in the London market and by flights of short-term funds from the United States to European financial centers. Though the situation has since improved somewhat, confidence in the dollar exchange rate has not yet been fully restored.

Our experience since 1960 illustrates dramatically how considerations relating to the state of a nation's balance of payments and international reserves can inhibit its efforts to promote maximum employment and growth at home. Our problem has been made especially difficult because the deficit in our balance of payments has continued despite the fact that most of the rest of the world has been in a boom while we have been in recession or, at best, in a state of incomplete recovery. Throughout this period the economies of most of western Europe have been operating close to capacity levels. This has justified relatively high interest rates in several European financial centers. Moreover, the high levels of real income in Europe have supported high levels of demand for imports, including imports from the United States. In this country, however, conditions have been far different. First we had the recession of 1960–61, and then a weak and incomplete recovery. At no time during this entire period has unemployment been as low as 5 per cent, and most of the time it has been much higher. This was clearly a period in which the domestic objectives of promoting employment and growth called for an expansionary monetary policy, an expansionary fiscal policy, or both. Yet any actions which would effectively promote these domestic objectives would tend to widen the deficit in our balance of payments and perhaps lower confidence in the dollar.

A really aggressive, expansionary monetary policy became doubly dangerous. To the extent that it lowered interest rates and especially short-term interest rates, it would widen the gap between rates here and in western European financial centers and stimulate further outflows of short-term funds. And what started as capital outflows induced by interest-rate differentials could generate lack of confidence in the stability of the dollar exchange rate and induce capital flights. Moreover, any expansionary policy, whether monetary or fiscal, that succeeded in raising our level of employment and output would tend to increase our balance-of-payments deficit by increasing our imports. With larger real output and income we would buy abroad both more raw materials to feed our production processes and more finished goods. The deficit would be further widened if our attempts to raise employment and output induced further increases of wages and prices. Such increases of domestic costs and prices would tend both to decrease our exports and increase our imports.

In short, our problems of promoting maximum employment and growth have become much more complex during the past three years. Before 1960, our efforts to promote growth and employment by increasing aggregate demand were inhibited only by our desire to avoid the domestic consequences of price inflation. Now we face, in addition, urgent and restrictive considerations relating to our balance of payments. There can be little doubt that this has been a major reason for our failure to take more aggressive expansionary actions to remedy the high rate of unemployment and the slow rate of growth during the past three years.

Is this perplexing situation merely temporary? Will our balance-of-payments and international reserve positions soon improve enough to restore in large measure our freedom to concentrate on domestic objectives? Perhaps so. Recalling that only a few years ago many were forecasting a chronic dollar shortage, one hesitates to forecast a chronic dollar glut. For example, the current inflationary pressures in western Europe may rescue us at least temporarily by enabling us to increase our exports and decrease our imports. But we cannot afford to be too optimistic. I think it more likely that it will be a long time before our balance-of-payments and international reserve positions will again be such as to give us the degree of freedom to pursue domestic objectives that we enjoyed for so many years before 1960.

There are, of course, many types of actions relative to balances of payments and international reserves that can be taken to increase our freedom to pursue domestic objectives. In a later paper my colleague, Professor Machlup, discusses various measures of international economic co-operation that would help us and other nations promote economic objectives. But many of these, as well as unilateral actions that we might take, involve choices among objectives, some highly important, others less so. For example, we might restrict imports by raising tariffs or imposing quantitative restrictions, but this would invite retaliation and conflict with our objective of expanding world trade and increasing the efficiency of the world's economy. We could reduce sharply, or even discontinue, our foreign-aid program, but this would conflict with our humanitarian and national-security objectives. We might restrict outflows of short-term capital, long-term capital, or both, but this would present serious enforcement problems and also conflict with our objective of promoting the free international flow of capital to increase the efficiency of the world's economy. We might also secure greater freedom to follow expansionary domestic policies by lowering the exchange rate on the dollar, which would make our exports less expensive to the rest of the world and our imports more expensive. However, one can confidently predict that this action will not be taken by the United States except as an almost last resort. Some of the objections to devaluation of the dollar are largely emotional and should not be weighed heavily. But there are also very substantial objections to such an action. To mention only one, devaluation of this great key currency, which is a major component of the international reserves of other countries, could do serious damage to the world's monetary system. For this and other reasons I hope that the present exchange rate on the dollar can be maintained. But the cost of maintaining a fixed exchange rate can be excessive, and the cost can be in the form of unemployment and a sluggish growth rate.

Such, in brief outline, is the history of our efforts since World War II to promote maximum employment and production. Let us now look to the future and try to identify some of the major problems that we are likely to encounter in our efforts to promote stability and growth. One thing is clear: aggregate demand and actual output will have to rise far above present levels if we are to avoid excessive and growing levels of unemployment. Output is at the present time considerably below capacity levels and unemployment considerably above the minimum levels necessitated by labor-market frictions. On top of this, our capacity to produce is rising rapidly. The size of our labor force will grow at a rapid pace, especially during the second half of this decade, as the large numbers born in the early postwar years reach the working age. Moreover, continuing technological change and other forces increasing output per man-hour will continue to reduce the demand for labor relative to output. Thus we face the problem of creating enough new jobs to absorb those now unemployed, the large group of new additions to the labor force, and those who will become disemployed by continuing technological advances. To achieve this will require continuously large increases in aggregate demand and actual output.

As we attempt to solve this set of problems we shall almost certainly continue to concern ourselves with multiple objectives and conflicts among them. We shall continue to debate about maximum employment, economic growth, price-level stability, and considerations relating to our balance-of-payments and international reserve positions. To devise and administer a combination of policies that will reconcile these objectives in some optimum way will challenge our ingenuity.

I believe that one of the most difficult tasks, as well as one of the most crucial, is that of securing a more satisfactory response of real output to increases of aggregate demand. We must find some way to avoid price increases and excessive wage increases while unemployment is still above the minimum levels necessitated by frictions in labor markets. Even perfect control of the behavior of aggregate demand will not enable us to reconcile our objectives satisfactorily if average money wage rates rise more rapidly than average output per man-hour. With average output per man-hour rising only about 2 or 2.5 per cent a year, more rapid increases of average wage rates inevitably raise costs of production and induce price increases.

Will this problem bedevil us in the future? For about three years now, prices have been almost stable and wage rates have been rising less rapidly than before. Some observers are much encouraged by this recent experience and believe this problem is now behind us. Perhaps it is. But we should remember that this has been a period in which unemployment has been continuously far above minimum levels. I fear that if we raise aggregate demand enough to eradicate this excess unemployment, we shall see a resumption of the upward wage-cost-price movements.

What specifically should we do to make real output more responsive to increases in aggregate demand and to avoid excessive wage increases while unemployment is still above minimum levels? There are few of us indeed who think it either politically feasible or economically desirable to have formal government control of wages, which would almost inevitably lead to detailed controls of the structure, as well as the general level, of wages and also to controls of prices. At the other extreme, there is little reason to expect success from a series of general, vague admonitions to unions and employers to "be good," "show restraint," and "remember the public interest." Such vague exhortations without any guiding principles are likely to be ineffective; and if effective, to be arbitrary and harmful.

In its report in January of 1962 the Council of Economic Advisers made a proposal which, I believe, deserves favorable consideration. Briefly, the Council proposed that before the beginning of each year the Council or some other responsible body should present a projection of economic conditions for that year and a proposed set of guidelines for wage behavior. These guidelines would indicate the type of wage behavior that would be most conducive to promoting the nation's economic objectives. Both the data and the guidelines would then be subjected to close scrutiny and full discussion by outside economists and by employers, unions, and others. Out of this process should come a better understanding of the facts and issues involved, and some guidelines for those who engage in wage bargaining and for those who judge the process and results.

One cannot forecast how successful such a program would be. To evolve suitable guidelines is no easy task. Moreover, there is no assurance that the behavior of employers and unions would be much affected. But surely the results would not be worse than those of the present situation, in which we have no guidelines based on rational economic analysis and little public understanding of the facts and issues involved.

We should also recognize that there are some types of unemployment that will not respond satisfactorily to even the most precise control of aggregate demand. I refer to the unemployed left in regions abandoned by industries or those whose occupations have been made obsolete by decreased demand for their products or by changes in technology. These unemployed obviously cannot find employment if aggregate demand is insufficient to create enough job opportunities, but there may be no level of aggregate demand which is desirable on other grounds that would draw them into employment. More specific measures are required to inform them of job opportunities, to retrain them, and to assist in their relocation. Our efforts of this type have been far too limited, but such programs as have been instituted have demonstrated their value to the country as a whole, as well as to the unemployed. They can make both employment and output respond more favorably to increases in aggregate demand.

In presenting the last two points I have argued that even if we achieved the most accurate control of aggregate demand for output, we would still need to adopt other measures to promote more favorable responses of employment and output. But we still have far to go before achieving such an accurate control of aggregate demand. There are several reasons for this, but I shall concentrate on only one: an inadequate use of fiscal policy for stabilization uses. Like many others, I believe we have relied too heavily on monetary policy and that our fiscal policies have lacked flexibility, timeliness, and power. This was true even before 1960, when our pursuit of domestic objectives was unhindered by considerations relating to our balance of payments. It applies with special force to situations such as we have had during the past three years, when considerations relating to our balance-of-payments and international reserve positions have been in the forefront. This has inhibited our use of monetary policy to increase aggregate demand and eradicate excessive unemployment, for an expansionary monetary policy aggressive enough to achieve these purposes would lower our interest-rate structure markedly, encourage capital outflows, and perhaps seriously damage confidence in the stability of the dollar in exchange markets. It may well be true, as many have alleged, that the Federal Reserve has allowed itself to be too much inhibited by these international considerations. Yet these dangers are indeed real, and I am convinced that in this environment the Federal Reserve could not safely have adopted monetary policies expansionary enough to achieve its domestic objectives. What has been needed for some time now is an expansionary fiscal policy in the form of tax reduction, an increase in government expenditures, or both—measures that would increase aggregate demand without necessitating decreased interest rates. But we have not yet had a tax reduction, and such increases in government expenditures as have occurred were adopted largely for other reasons and have been too small to induce the necessary rise of aggregate demand. For all this, we have been paying and continue to pay a high price in terms of excessive unemployment and a gross national product tens of billions below capacity levels.

If fiscal policies are to contribute more toward promoting our economic stabilization objectives, we shall have to solve several difficult problems. One is to achieve more general agreement both within and outside the government that the promotion of economic stability should be a major objective of fiscal policy. This is not to say that economic stability should be the only objective of our tax and expenditure policies. We must continue to be concerned with equity in the distribution of tax burdens, the social usefulness of the government's substantive programs, the allocation of resources between the private and public sectors, efficiency in both sectors, and so on. But these other important objectives are not irreconcilable with that of promoting economic stability, and we need to make sure that our concern for them does not lead us to downgrade or neglect our stabilization goals.

We shall also have to achieve a better understanding, both within and outside the government, as to the types of fiscal policies required to promote economic stability. As indicated earlier, this involves repudiation of a fiscal rule that still commands the loyalty of many influential people—the rule of an annually balanced budget. Many still believe that the appearance of a large budget surplus should always be countered by a tax cut or an increase in government expenditures and that a large budget deficit should always be eradicated by tax increases or decreased government expenditures.

One must respect the basic motivations of those who advocate an annually balanced budget; they seek to promote fiscal responsibility and efficiency in government. I only wish that this simple and easily understood rule of thumb would indeed give us the results we seek. But the fact is that it will often produce or accentuate economic instability. Deficits will often occur when aggregate demand for output is inadequate. Tax increases or decreases in government expenditures at such times will magnify the inadequacy of demand. Also, surpluses in the budget may often occur when aggregate demand is excessive. Tax cuts or increases in government expenditures at such times would accentuate inflationary pressures. Thus the simple rule of an annually balanced budget is unacceptable. However, as this rule is abandoned we shall have to develop and secure general understanding and acceptance of new principles to promote fiscal responsibility and efficiency. This will be difficult, but it is both possible and essential.

As we achieve greater understanding and more general agreement as to the types of fiscal policies that will best promote our objectives, the timeliness and flexibility of fiscal actions should be improved. Congress itself may be able to move more quickly and appropriately, with less delay and controversy. And it might delegate to the President, with appropriate instructions and safeguards, limited powers to change taxes, expenditures, or both.

Now for the summing up. Our attempts to promote economic stability in the period since World War II can, I think, be judged a qualified success. We have avoided a major depression; our recessions have been shallow and short; our real output has grown markedly; and since 1951 the rate of price increases has been kept within tolerable bounds. But we have no reason for complacency. The record to date has left much to be desired. We have not yet reached enduring solutions to basic problems relating both to objectives and to methods of implementation. We have not yet adjusted to our new international economic position that has emerged as the economies of other industrialized countries have recovered and prospered, freedom of international capital movements has been restored, and our balance-of-payments and international reserve positions have deteriorated. We cannot foresee other environmental changes that the future will bring, but it is safe to predict that they will be numerous and important. For example, technological changes will almost certainly continue to be rapid and important. The whole international monetary mechanism built around gold exchange standards may prove to be defective and to require far-reaching reforms, if it is not to interfere with our efforts to promote economic stability. And it may well turn out, as Per Jacobssen of the International Monetary Fund has warned us, that in the coming years economic forces will be predominantly toward deflation rather than inflation. We must be prepared for the possibility that the task of promoting economic stability will become more difficult rather than less so. This task is well begun, but it is far from finished.

ARTHUR F. BURNS

Economics and Our Public Policy
of Full Employment

D URING the nineteenth century, full employment was just a dream of a small band of reformers. Today it is a firmly established objective of public policy through the greater part of the world, including our own country. The Employment Act, which was passed by the Congress in 1946, states plainly that it is the continuing responsibility of the federal government to create and maintain "conditions under which there will be afforded useful employment opportunities, including self-employment, for those able, willing, and seeking to work."[1] This moral commitment to full employment has been reaffirmed time and again by successive Presidents and successive Congresses. There can be no doubt that it expresses faithfully the prevailing sentiment of the American people. What we debate nowadays is the scale, the timing, and the precise character of employment policies, not the need to strive for full employment or to use the powers of government to move the nation towards this goal.

The pursuit of full employment has naturally served to enhance the role of economists in the formation of public policy.[2] Government officials charged with the responsibility of administering the Employment Act need to know how economic trends have been developing. They need to form judgments about the demand for labor and its supply in the months or years ahead. They need to shape or readjust policies to relieve existing unemployment. They need to devise ways of minimizing unemployment in the future. In view of the frailty of

ARTHUR F. BURNS is John Bates Clark Professor of Economics at Columbia University and President of the National Bureau of Economic Research.

[1] This Act, except for recent minor amendments, is conveniently reproduced in *Economic Report of the President* (January, 1954), Appendix B.

[2] See "An Economist in Government" by the present writer, *Columbia University Forum* (Winter, 1957).

much of economic knowledge, the economist cannot often speak with the impersonal authority of science on these vital matters. His power to predict the future is as yet very limited. As is true of other men, his economic judgments are influenced by ethical intuitions and philosophical attitudes. These limitations of economics and of economists must be understood. It is well, however, not to underestimate the power of economics to define and disentangle the issues with which policymakers are concerned. If economists cannot be implicitly trusted to lead the nation to the goal of full employment, they can at least clarify the nature of the goal and the obstacles that may be encountered by taking this or that route to it.

I intend to take advantage of the quiet setting of Rice University by discussing some issues surrounding the goal of full employment. I do so in the belief that a clearer notion of what full employment means may help our nation to deal with its unemployment—a problem which President Kennedy has recently characterized as "our number one economic problem."[3]

Causes of Unemployment

The causes of unemployment are complex and many. We usually associate it with business recessions or a lagging rate of economic growth, and we are apt nowadays to attribute both the one and the other to a deficiency of aggregate demand. However, even if the business cycle vanished, a troublesome volume of unemployment would remain.

In the first place, seasonal variations of economic activity will continue. At certain seasons of the year, a considerable number of workers will still be laid off or lose their jobs in the construction industry, in the garment trades, in the automobile industry, in vacation resorts, and in many other places and activities.[4]

In the second place, the fortunes of individual firms, industries, and communities will still vary enormously. The economic impact on working people will therefore be uneven. Here and there, men and women will become unemployed as new technology renders their skills obsolete, or as factories move to new locations, as old mines become exhausted, as construction projects reach completion, or as both old and new businesses shut down or reduce their operations because

---

[3] *Manpower Report of the President* (March, 1963), p. xi.

[4] It is perhaps worth noting that the seasonal corrections of monthly figures of unemployment, as practiced by statisticians, merely redistribute the unemployment that occurs within a year. They do not serve to reduce the annual level of the figures. Nor should they do so; this function belongs to economic policy, not to statistical contrivance.

they are unable to compete successfully against their rivals. Inevitably, some interval often elapses before those who have lost jobs can find employment once again.

In the third place, the disappearance of the business cycle will not of itself eradicate certain differences among people that count in our labor markets. In all probability, the rate of unemployment will therefore remain higher for young persons than for the labor force at large, for Negroes than for native whites, for women than for men, for older workers than for those in the prime of life, for those with little schooling than for educated persons, for the physically handicapped than for those free from disability, and for lethargic people than for those who proceed with energy and initiative. Needless to add, the rate of unemployment will also be higher for men and women who harbor somewhat romantic notions about their worth than for those who adjust readily to market conditions.

The significance of these familiar observations should be clear. What they mean is that a risk of unemployment is present for the individual even in times of prosperity, that whether times are good or bad the risk is uneven for different parts of the working population, that this risk increases materially during business recessions, and that it may remain uncomfortably large when economic recovery proceeds slowly. These are reasons enough for public policy to concern itself with unemployment. But if the goal of full employment is to be of constructive aid in diminishing unemployment, it must be framed with an eye to actual characteristics of people and the conditions under which they live and work.

Full Employment and Other Values

In popular discussions, the goal of full employment is sometimes described in phrases that are so sweeping as to suggest that it would be well if every man, woman, and child worked twenty-four hours every day. Of course, no one wants or means that. Everyone recognizes the infirmities of childhood and old age, that human endurance has its limits, that much of leisure is sanctioned by custom or religion, and that a free society leaves it up to an individual to decide whether to work or not. When we speak precisely, we do not therefore identify the unemployed with the jobless. Instead, we consider as unemployed only those among the jobless who are able, willing, and seeking to work. If all persons of this category actually succeeded in finding jobs, employment would surely be at a maximum while unemployment would disappear.

This seems to be the objective of public leaders when they assert, as men often do in a mood of exuberance, that the elimination of unemployment is a basic goal of our society. For example, the Council of Economic Advisers recently declared that "ideally, all persons able, willing, and seeking to work should be continuously employed."[5] Statements such as this convey a noble sentiment, but they can hardly be taken literally. I doubt if anyone who has seriously thought about the matter really believes that the complete elimination of unemployment would be ideal or even good for our type of society, in contrast to one that is rigidly governed by custom or authority.

We can put what I say to a test by a little reflection. Let us provisionally agree that full employment means a condition of zero unemployment. This, let us say, is the goal towards which public policy should be directed. Let us suppose, next, that the rate of governmental spending is sharply increased in the interest of stimulating the economy and that a large and well-sustained upsurge of private spending follows. Employment in most lines of activity will therefore rise progressively, unemployment will diminish, and the economy will move towards the established goal. As the process of expansion gathers momentum, young men and women embarking on their careers will find it easier to obtain suitable work; members of minority groups and many of the physically handicapped will discover that they and their services are wanted; and not a few women who took jobs because their husbands were temporarily out of work will resume their normal family responsibilities. Hence, there will be ample cause for satisfaction in the improved performance of our economy.

Prosperity, however, has a habit of creating problems of its own. When the demand for all sorts of commodities and services steadily increases and unemployment decreases, costs of production and prices do not stand still. In the early stages of expansion, increases of output can commonly be achieved without significant addition to overhead costs. As output keeps growing, this source of economy diminishes and eventually vanishes. Technological and managerial advances continue, of course, to be made at a thousand points. Their favorable influence on costs is offset, however, as older equipment is again put to use, as the quality of newly hired labor declines, as hours of work lengthen and overtime rates are paid, as fatigue grips both managers and their employees, as workers become more restless and independent, and as deliveries of needed materials or equipment become less dependable.

These developments would in time raise costs of production even if wage rates remained constant. That, however, will not happen.

[5] *Economic Report of the President* (January, 1962), p. 44.

With aggregate demand continuing to expand, labor shortages will appear first in this trade or community, then in another, and so keep multiplying. Wages will therefore rise on a wide front, and they would do so even if trade unions were few and weak. Prices will likewise rise under the pressure of expanding demand, sometimes advancing before, and sometimes after, wages have risen.

Not all of us, of course, will be troubled by the higher prices that now have to be paid for consumer goods. Indeed, most of us may point with pride to the power of our economic system to provide employment for more and more people who are less fortunate than we, but who also want to live decently, raise families, and give their children a good start in life. Many of us will have a more personal cause for rejoicing—either because our incomes have risen faster than the cost of living or because the market value of our holdings of common stocks or real estate has soared. There will be some among us, however, whose savings have been accumulated chiefly in the form of bank deposits, savings bonds, or life insurance. There will be others, too, whose salaries or wages have failed to keep in step with the rise in the cost of living. There will be still others whose livelihood depends on a pension, annuity, or some other type of fixed income. These groups will not be indifferent to the rise of prices. Nor will economists, public officials, and others who ponder the future as they watch speculation spreading, economic injustices multiplying, the balance of payments deteriorating, and—perhaps also—the world's confidence in the dollar declining.

The advance of costs and prices will therefore arouse some skepticism about the ideal of full employment that we postulated. Symptoms of shortage, besides that of soaring prices, will add their mite to this changing mood.[6] In view of the scarcity of labor, more and more of us will find that we must deal with a salesgirl whose understanding is faulty, or that we must get along with a janitor who seems never to be around, or that we must defer to the plumber who arrives a week after we had discovered a leaky pipe, or that we must learn to wait patiently for the new sofa that was promised for the wedding anniversary we celebrated three months earlier. So great is the variety of human nature and of personal circumstance that, notwithstanding the persisting advance of prices and the mounting of personal inconvenience, there will still be some among us who continue to espouse with fervor the goal of zero unemployment. But there will now be others, and their number is likely to swell as the expansion of aggregate demand becomes more intense, who will not only question the

[6] Cf. Bertil Ohlin, *The Problem of Employment Stabilization* (New York: Columbia University Press, 1949), chap. 1.

practical wisdom of their earlier ideal but will actually complain that the economy is suffering from overfull employment.

Once this stage has been reached, the simple concept of full employment with which we started will have lost its usefulness for public policy. True, all or most of us may still believe sincerely in full employment, but this will now mean different things to us, reflecting our individual values, attitudes, and circumstances. Compassion for the unemployed will weigh heavily in the scales, but other values will also count—among them a concern about the cost of living, industrial efficiency, the rate of economic growth, the scope of governmental authority, the level of taxes, the balance of payments, the prestige of our country abroad, to say nothing of such earthly matters as personal convenience in riding trains or shopping. This diversity of values is, of course, the condition in which we find ourselves in actual life, and it is one reason why economists, among others, differ in the advice they give to lawmakers.

FUNCTIONS OF SOME UNEMPLOYMENT

If my analysis has run close to the track of human sentiment, it follows that zero unemployment, apart from being unattainable,[7] would not really be a desirable condition for our society. But if that much is true, we should recognize that not all unemployment is evil, and that some unemployment actually serves a useful function from the viewpoint of the individual or that of society. Although this proposition may appear strange to some of you, let us consider the case for it.

To begin with, some of the unemployment experienced by young men and women when they look for their first regular job is linked to our national tradition of freedom. Having a job is obviously important to them, and there are times when any job is better than none. Ordinarily, however, some picking and choosing helps young people to decide what they would like to do and how they can make the most of their capabilities. This, of course, results in a certain amount of unemployment. The only conceivable way of avoiding it would be to have young people take the very first job that came along. Such

---

[7] Popular impressions to the contrary, some unemployment has persisted even in the U.S.S.R. See Warren W. Eason, "Labor Force Materials for the Study of Unemployment in the Soviet Union," and the discussion of this in *The Measurement and Behavior of Unemployment* (Special Conference 8, Universities-National Bureau Committee for Economic Research [Princeton, N.J.: Princeton University Press for National Bureau of Economic Research, 1957]); also, I. Kaplan, "A Questionnaire Study of the Causes of Labor Turnover in the Industry of the Economic Councils," *Problems of Economics* (IASP Translations from Original Soviet Sources) [December, 1961], pp. 42–47.

a rule of conduct would hardly recommend itself to them or, for that matter, to older men and women when they decide to re-enter the labor force.

Unemployment arises voluntarily also among those who already have jobs. Independent businessmen sometimes discontinue one business before they establish another. Employees frequently leave their jobs before they have found new work. Some workers quit because they become dissatisfied with the rate of pay; or because they see no opportunity or insufficient opportunity for advancement; or because they do not like their work, or their working conditions, or the neighborhood where they live. Others leave because they think that their talents can be put to better use elsewhere; or because they wish to try out different jobs, or live in different places before settling down; or because they are moved to sudden anger by a foreman's or colleague's injury to their feelings; or because they decide to seek or to follow husbands, wives, or sweethearts. Migration from job to job occurs at all stages of life, but it is especially common among young folk, who have both more opportunity and better reason for experimenting. To the extent that unemployment arises from the striving of men and women to escape the limitations of one environment and to seek out the opportunities of another, we may justly regard it as useful both to the individual and to society.

But if the exercise of freedom by new job seekers or by established employees creates some unemployment, so also does the exercise of freedom by employers. Individual employees are undoubtedly injured in the process. This fact warrants steady search for constructive ways of easing personal adjustments, but it should not blind us to the advantages that accrue to society from the exercise of freedom. In every group enterprise—whether it be a business firm, a government bureau, or a university—a certain degree of discipline is essential if the efforts of the group are to prosper. Individuals who are incompetent, undependable, or dishonest must be subject to the risk of dismissal, or else order and efficiency will suffer. Moreover, we could not have an efficient economy if employers who closed down their shops were required to support in idleness the men who previously worked for them, or if those who remained in business but needed fewer workers —whether because of dwindling markets or of technological changes— still had to retain their earlier work force on the payroll.

Industrial efficiency depends not only on the maintenance of certain standards of job performance and on the ability of every enterprise to dispense with labor that is no longer needed. Industrial efficiency depends also on the ability of an enterprise to maintain smooth operations and to meet unforeseen contingencies. We have already seen how the normal activities of consumption are impeded when un-employment tends to vanish. But if inability to locate a plumber, or a laborer, or a spare part may cause trouble or inconvenience to house-holds, it will also impede the efficiency of business firms. Just as stocks of raw materials help to insure the continuity of production, so does the existence of a certain number of people seeking work help to in-sure the continuity and efficiency of production and thereby also con-tributes to the stability of total employment itself.[8]

The upshot of these remarks is simply that some unemployment is necessary or desirable from the viewpoint of a society that values freedom, equity, and efficiency. More specifically, we must have some unemployment if new entrants into the labor force are to be free to choose among jobs, if employed individuals are to be free to change jobs, if employers are to be free to replace unsatisfactory workers or to dispense with those whose services they no longer require, if busi-ness firms are to be able to carry on their productive operations with reasonable continuity and efficiency, and if the purchasing power of the dollar is to maintain some semblance of stability.

MINIMUM RATE OF UNEMPLOYMENT

These broad but basic considerations may be stressed differently by individual economists. All economists recognize, however, that if the concept of full employment is to serve public policy constructive-ly, it must at least allow for seasonal variations in economic activity and for the familiar frictions of the labor market. Since the adoption of the Employment Act, economists have also been under pressure to add precision to the concept of full employment. This has proved to be a difficult and sometimes a very disconcerting task.[9]

An obvious starting point of the quest for precision is the Act's specification of the goal of "maximum employment." Some students have reasoned that since the Act takes maximum employment as the objective of public policy, it is desirable—even if not strictly neces-sary—to express this magnitude numerically. Others have gone fur-ther and argued that unless the objective of full employment is ex-pressed by a definite number, policymakers will not know the magni-tude of the gap in activity that needs to be filled and therefore will be unable to devise satisfactory public policies. In line with this thinking, the Council of Economic Advisers declared in its Report of March,

[8] The need of continuity could, of course, be met in part by hoarding labor, but only at the cost of efficiency and the fluidity required for growth. See also pp. 65–66 in this connection.

[9] See E. G. Nourse, "Defining our Employment Goal under the 1946 Act," *Review of Economics and Statistics*, XXXVIII (May, 1956).

1961, that an unemployment rate of 4 per cent is a reasonable target for full utilization of resources.[10] In this pronouncement the Council merely used a figure which had gradually become something of a convention in economic circles during the postwar period. The Council, however, took the novel step of making this figure official.

The use of a 4 per cent unemployment rate as a criterion of full employment in our country can be rationalized in different ways. One possible justification is that when unemployment has been at that level or lower, it does not appear to have been much of a political problem. This argument will hardly satisfy those who believe that the American people need to apply a more exacting standard to the performance of their economy. Another possible justification is that the average unemployment rate during peak years of the business cycle works out for the period since 1900 to a figure that is close to 4 per cent.[11] This historical generalization is surely not irrelevant to a practical judgment concerning full employment, but it too will not satisfy those whose hearts are set on a different numerical goal. After all, there is nothing sacred about an average, especially when it varies with the precise period covered and with the treatment accorded to extreme cases, such as the war peak in 1918 or the depressed peak in 1937. Those who deem a 4 per cent unemployment rate too high can always point to historical instances when the rate was lower, while those who deem 4 per cent too low can point to inflationary conditions in years when the rate was at that level or even higher.

Of course, criticism of the 4 per cent figure along these lines is not directed against the desirability of numerical targets as such. But if what I said previously about the subtle role of human attitudes and values is valid, any unemployment rate that identifies full employment in the minds of people at one time may fail to do so at another time, for example, if prices begin rising swiftly. On this view, the presence or absence of full employment must be judged with reference to the entire complex of conditions that bear on a nation's economic health.

Still another criticism is that it really makes little difference whether the unemployment target is, say, 3 or 5 per cent. The point here is that the two figures are very close, that they imply an employment target of either 97 or 95 per cent, and that the economy will be doing about as well at one level of activity as at the other. This way

[10] *Hearings on January 1961 Economic Report of the President, Joint Economic Committee* (87th Cong., 1st sess.), p. 326.

[11] Based on official data and Stanley Lebergott, "Annual Estimates of Unemployment in the United States, 1900–1950," in *The Measurement and Behavior of Unemployment* (cited in n. 7), pp. 215–16.

of thinking must appear strange, if not irresponsible, to those who see and judge the economic world in terms of its unemployment. To them it makes a great deal of difference where the unemployment target is set. According to their lights, if unemployment happens to be 5 per cent, then the distance from full employment will be twice as large with a target of 3 per cent as with one of 4 per cent. One who believes that compelling human or economic factors favor 3 per cent can therefore urge with a show of plausibility that whatever increase of governmental spending is being proposed to move the economy to the 4 per cent goal is merely half of what is required.

In view of the rich diversity of such judgments, it is not surprising that a storm of criticism from both the left and the right followed the Council's announcement that a 4 per cent rate of unemployment is a reasonable goal for full utilization of the nation's resources. The Council responded by explaining that the figure is simply "an interim goal, a way-station."[12] Needless to say, this modification will also not satisfy everyone, although the nebulous part of the new official goal is perhaps its strongest feature. The crucial weakness of the Council's 4 per cent figure is not that it is arbitrary. On the contrary, this figure is sufficiently grounded in experience to be useful on many occasions. The difficulty is rather that any numerical goal of full employment, once it has been made official, can be easily misinterpreted and become an obstacle to rational economic policy in a changing world.[13] For instance, if several hundred thousand teenagers or women suddenly entered the labor force and sought temporary, part-time jobs, unemployment could jump from 4 to 5 per cent but that would have little economic significance and require no change in public policy. On the other hand, even an unemployment rate of 3 per cent could be dangerous to a nation if it rose to that level in the course of a new recession. The threat at such a time would not be the unemployment that exists, but rather the cumulating force of recession that could in time carry unemployment to 6 or 8 per cent or even higher.

Criteria of Full Employment

There is no need to dwell further on the point that full employment cannot be wisely identified with a fixed numerical target. This conclusion, however, will not make life easier for the makers of federal economic policy. True, it may help them avoid some costly mis-

---

[12] See *Economic Report of the President* (January, 1963), p. 42; also *ibid.* (January, 1962), pp. 44–48.

[13] Cf. my comments in *Hearings on January 1955 Economic Report of the President, Joint Committee on the Economic Report* (84th Cong., 1st sess.), pp. 43–45.

takes, but they also need positive assistance in interpreting their duties under the Employment Act.

As far as I know, there are only two passages in the Act that give any promise of eventually bringing some precision to its employment objective. One is the specification of the goal of "maximum employment" which, as we have just seen, easily leads to unhappy arithmetical debates. But the Act also specifies, as I noted at the beginning of this lecture, that the federal government has the responsibility of promoting conditions that will afford "useful employment opportunities . . . for those able, willing, and seeking to work."[14] This passage does not invite absolute numerical targets of employment or of the unemployment rate. It will not suit those who seek the illusory comfort of precise targets. It nevertheless provides, in my judgment, a more useful handle for a public policy of full employment.

The central thought of this passage of the Employment Act is simply that ample employment opportunities are of great social or public importance. Let us now pursue this thought in the light of our earlier conclusion that some unemployment is socially desirable. That conclusion rested on a tacit assumption which very much needs to be made explicit, namely, that unfilled jobs exist. Clearly, new entrants into the labor force will be unable to exercise their freedom to choose among jobs if there are no jobs to be filled. Nor will those at work be able to exercise their freedom to change jobs if there are no vacancies. Nor, speaking more generally, will those who are seeking jobs, whatever the cause of their searching, be able to get work unless jobs are being created or vacated. It follows that job opportunities—or, more narrowly, vacant jobs—are absolutely vital. It further follows that if the number of job vacancies equaled the number unemployed, there would then be sufficient employment opportunities to permit, in principle, a job for all who are able, willing, and seeking to work.

This line of reasoning leads at once to a basic criterion of full employment, namely, equality between the number of jobs seeking men and the number of men seeking jobs. Of course, these quantities need to be considered in terms of the market place. If the prevailing wage in a given trade happened to be approximately twenty dollars a day, it would make little sense to treat a man who holds out for thirty dollars as being unemployed. It would likewise be pointless to treat an employer who is willing to pay only ten dollars as having a real vacancy. In other words, we need to think of the relation between unemployment and job vacancies in terms of actual market conditions. Furthermore, we need to recognize that it makes a good deal of difference to the general welfare, and therefore also to public policy,

14 See n. 1.

whether equality between the number of unemployed and the number of job vacancies comes to rest at a figure of three million or thirteen million. Taking all these considerations together, full employment may be said to mean that the number of vacant jobs at prevailing wages is as large as the number unemployed and that the labor market is so organized that everyone who is able, willing, and seeking to work already has a job or can obtain one after a brief search or after undergoing some training.[15]

Let us now see how helpful this interpretation of full employment can be in formulating public policy. First of all, the criterion of equality between the number of unemployed and the number of vacant jobs poses squarely what in the economic sphere is perhaps the major policy problem of our generation, namely, whether aggregate demand at a particular time is deficient and, if so, what action the government can wisely take. Many of us have become accustomed to attribute every drop in general economic activity—more recently also every sign of sluggishness in the rate of economic growth—to a deficiency of aggregate demand, and we are therefore apt to urge the government to compensate for any deficiency that we believe exists. This way of thinking is often sound, practically useful, and socially beneficial. It rests, however, on an excessively simple view of the economic process. There can surely be difficulties on the supply side as well as on the demand side; for example, when a protracted strike in a major industry or a concentration of geographical shifts of businesses brings economic trouble, including unemployment. In diagnosing the state of the economy, it is critically important therefore to check the

[15] Stated more formally, equality between the number of vacant jobs and the number unemployed is a necessary but not a sufficient condition of full employment. The two other conditions are, first, that the equality holds at prevailing wages, second, that the labor market is so organized that practically all of the unemployed could obtain a job after a brief search or after obtaining some special training. Cf. W. H. Beveridge, *Full Employment in a Free Society* (New York: W. W. Norton & Co., 1945), pp. 18–20, 124–31.

Equality of job openings and job seekers, at prevailing wages, could emerge at a high level of unemployment. In that event, the obstacle to full employment would not be the level of aggregate demand, but rather that the unemployed lack the highly intricate skills that are wanted, or that they choose not to practice them, or that they are located in the wrong places, or that they lack information about available jobs, or that legal wage minima are out of line with conditions in some markets. Even this statement is incomplete, for it assumes that adjustments must be on the side of supply, whereas some could in fact be made by those demanding specific types of labor.

The present concept of the goal of full employment would require for its full implementation detailed statistics on the structure (occupational, geographic, sex, age, etc.) as well as on the over-all level of both job vacancies and unemployment. However, even if we had nothing more than national totals, we would still be able to judge whether or not existing unemployment was due to a deficiency of aggregate demand. In deciding this issue, both job vacancies and unemployment would need to be expressed in seasonally adjusted form.

number unemployed against the number of job vacancies before concluding that aggregate demand has become deficient or to what degree this has happened.

Let me be more specific. I think that informed citizens will generally agree that our economy has suffered in recent years from excessive unemployment. There is less agreement, however, about the causes of the unemployment or the proper remedy for it. According to one school of thought—I shall call it the expansionist school—the principal cause is a more or less chronic shortage of aggregate demand. According to another school of thought—to which I shall refer as the structural school—the principal cause is found in the rapid piling up of economic changes, which have been creating more jobs than can be filled in some occupations and communities while substantial unemployment is being created in others.

Each school has presented impressive evidence to support its position, but neither the one nor the other has been able to demonstrate conclusively that its diagnosis is the right one. Thus the expansionist school stresses the recent failure of business investment in fixed capital to match earlier economic performance, the reduced rate of growth of total production since 1957, and the higher rate of unemployment since then. These facts may be granted; but they still leave open the vital question whether the number unemployed has been larger or smaller than the job vacancies. Unless this question is resolved, there is bound to be at least some lingering doubt about the characteristic remedy of the expansionist school—namely, easy credit, larger federal expenditures, lower tax rates, or some combination of these policies for increasing aggregate demand.

The structural school, in its turn, stresses the existence of extensive shortages of scientists, teachers, engineers, doctors, nurses, typists, stenographers, automobile and TV mechanics, tailors, domestic servants, and some other types of labor. In view of these shortages, it denounces the fiscal remedies proposed by the expansionists as being circuitous and needlessly costly. A far more effective way of dealing with unemployment, according to the structuralists, is to focus policy on better organization of the labor market—for example, by disseminating fuller and more timely reports on occupational trends, by bringing together pertinent data on every unemployed individual and every vacant job in a pool of information co-ordinated by employment exchanges,[16] by improving the existing system of vocational

---

[16] Electronic computers open up exciting possibilities for the future. With their aid, an unemployed worker expressing his need or preference to an officer of an employment exchange might be referred in a matter of hours, if not minutes, to a list of poten-

training and guidance, and by extending as soon as experience justifies it the retraining programs that have been established under recent legislation. All this and even more may be granted by the expansionists without budging from their position. They can properly insist that the mere existence of shortages in various occupations or communities by no means discredits their thesis that, taking the nation as a whole, unemployment substantially exceeds the unfilled jobs.[17]

These recent discussions have served to illustrate once again that inadequate knowledge of the causes of economic difficulty is by no means a bar to strong opinions on the part of economists or of others. This is unavoidable when a problem like unemployment, about which men feel deeply, becomes a subject of public concern. It is not so much the exaggeration by this or that school that I find deplorable, as the complete absence of national statistics on job vacancies. The Employment Act has now been on the statute books nearly twenty years. It has come to serve as a sort of "constitution" for economic policy making.[18] Its authority is constantly invoked by both public officials and private citizens. Its emphasis on ample employment opportunities is widely applauded. In its name all sorts of governmental programs are debated or undertaken to expand aggregate demand. Yet our nation has thus far failed to take the trouble to equip itself with the facts needed to determine whether, when, or to what degree, aggregate demand is deficient. If over-all national statistics on job vacancies existed, and if they were supported by data on job openings and unemployment in individual occupations and communities, much of the debate between the expansionists and the structuralists could be resolved on a factual basis.[19] Controversy about public policy would doubtless continue for reasons to which I have already alluded, but it would proceed along more constructive channels, concentrating on future prospects and needs of the economy—a subject on which men are bound to hold different opinions.

---

tial employers (outside his community if there are none in his own) who need that type of employee. Employers could be served in a similar way. If all this seems remote, the main reason is that our Federal-State Employment Service has failed to flourish.

[17] My own speculations on this issue, if of any interest in this connection, are expressed, among other places, in the Preface to Thomas B. Curtis, *87 Million Jobs* (New York: Duell, Sloan & Pierce, Inc., 1962), and in a statement at *Hearings on January 1963 Economic Report of the President, Joint Economic Committee* (88th Cong., 1st sess.).

[18] See A. F. Burns, "Some Reflections on the Employment Act," *Political Science Quarterly*, LXXVII (December, 1962).

[19] There is some reason to hope that the report of the Gordon Committee will be more successful than an earlier effort by the Council of Economic Advisers in getting a national system of job vacancy statistics organized. See President's Committee To Appraise Employment and Unemployment Statistics, *Measuring Employment and Unemployment* (September, 1962), pp. 25, 199–202, and Appendix B.

EFFECTIVENESS OF LABOR MARKETS

The concept of full employment that I have sketched may be helpful to policymakers also in other ways. By focusing on job opportunities as well as on job shortages, on employment as well as on unemployment, this concept should help to keep the healthy and the pathological aspects of economic life in perspective. Moreover, it should help to make students of public policy more alert to structural problems of our economy. As I have already noted, even if the business cycle vanished, unemployment would remain troublesome. Even if there were never any shortage of aggregate demand, the mutual adjustments of supply and demand for labor would often proceed slowly. Hence, whatever one may think of the merits of the controversy between the structuralists and the expansionists, there can be no doubt that unemployment would be very substantially reduced through better organization and functioning of the labor market.

This aspect of the unemployment problem has not received the attention it deserves on the part of economists. For example, economists frequently urge extension of the coverage of unemployment insurance and liberalization of benefits on the ground that such reforms would make the unemployment-insurance system a more powerful stabilizer of personal incomes and of consumer buying. This argument, which I think is valid, does not justify the tendency to neglect the supply side or the interaction of supply and demand. There is a serious need to revamp the insurance system so that more effective aid would be given to unemployed workers in finding new jobs. There is a need to devise ways of administration that would strictly withhold benefits from those who quit their jobs without good cause or who are unwilling to accept suitable work. There is a need to use the insurance system to enlarge the retraining opportunities for workers who can have little hope of finding employment in their own trade. It should also be possible to modify the insurance system so as to give employers a greater financial incentive to stabilize output. Structural reforms along these lines would promote better adjustment of the supply of labor to the prevailing demand. They would serve to prevent unemployment as well as to relieve it. Indeed, it is doubtful if the advantages sought from extended or liberalized insurance benefits will be realized unless they are accompanied by extensive structural reforms.[20]

Another problem that deserves the attention of economists is that while many workers have recently been unemployed or have had to

---

[20] Cf. the writer's comments in the *Proceedings of the Fourteenth Annual Meeting of the Industrial Relations Research Association* (December, 1961), pp. 198–200.

be content with part-time jobs, many others have been working over-time or holding down extra jobs. For manufacturing, accurate data exist on overtime and they disclose a disturbing development. In 1956, a year of booming business, overtime accounted for three hours of the average workweek. In 1962, when business activity was sluggish, overtime was equally abundant, although the number of manufactur-ing workers had in the meantime fallen by 8 per cent. One possible explanation of this increasing tendency to keep people on overtime is the steady growth of fringe benefits, the cost of which to a business firm tends to vary with the number of men employed rather than with the number of man-hours worked. Another possibility is that employers are gradually learning that disputes about work rules are fewer when they resort to overtime than when they add to their work force and therefore need to rearrange some of the jobs. These and other hypotheses require the most careful study by economists. For if it is really true that collective bargaining and some of our social legislation are tending to complicate the unemployment problem, it would be well to turn at once to exploring ways of reducing the dangerous side effects.

The very high unemployment rate among young people in recent years is still another problem that cannot be understood in its entirety in terms of the theory of deficient aggregate demand. More recog-nition needs to be given to what the increasing emphasis of our so-ciety on academic training and college education is doing to the minds of young people. The dignity of honest labor, whether skilled or unskilled, is no longer stressed by parents or teachers as it once was. Not all youngsters, however, are capable of climbing high on the competitive educational ladder. Some lack the interest, or the intelli-gence, or the emotional stability to do so. When they are told on all sides that life holds out little for a person who lacks a good education, it is not surprising that many young men and women, who could have become good workers at some trade, drop out of school and join the ranks of casual labor. Whatever the answer to this distressing problem may be, we can be quite sure that the mere expansion of aggregate demand will not solve it.

The main reason more attention has not been devoted to this and other peculiarities of labor markets is the preoccupation of economists with the problem of demand. The belief has developed and is now widely held that, whatever the cause or causes of unemployment may be, a sufficient increase of aggregate demand will in time work an effective cure. On an abstract plane this theory seems quite valid, as I in fact have shown by analyzing what would happen for a time if the government constantly kept injecting new money into the income stream. But I also concluded that demonstration by stressing the revulsion of feeling that would eventually be stirred by any such experiment.[21] There are limits to the amount of inflation, and the inefficiency and inconvenience associated with it, that our country will tolerate. Indeed, these limits are more severe in actual life than in my illustration. The practical significance of this is that the discontent aroused by a large inflationary experiment would be likely to lead to its discontinuance before enough of a dent had been made in structural unemployment.[22] Not only that, but massive political resistance could develop to any early repetition of the experiment even on the modest scale that might be needed to deal with that part of unemployment which, in the event of a recession, is really due to an insufficiency of aggregate demand.

I am well aware of the need for further research on the problem of business cycles and on the more general problem of maintaining aggregate demand at satisfactory levels. I surely hope that such research will go forward at Rice University and elsewhere. I particularly hope that economists will seek better understanding of the subtle forces that shape the confidence that businessmen, investors, and consumers have in their own and the nation's future. But I also feel that far more of the best thought of economists needs to be devoted to the several structural aspects of unemployment that I singled out for attention, as well as to related problems such as the influence of the minimum wage and current ways of administering welfare programs on the supply of labor, the influence of prejudice on the job opportunities of older men and minority groups, the effectiveness of both old and new training and retraining programs, the feasibility of reducing seasonal fluctuations in employment, and so on. If I am also right in thinking that comprehensive statistics on job vacancies are a vital missing link in our entire system of economic intelligence, there is plenty of useful work ahead for economists.[23]

It is by patient extension of the still small area of knowledge and understanding that economics has made its principal contribution to public policy in the past. That is also the way in which new usefulness to our public policy of full employment will be found in the future.

[21] See pp. 58–60 of this paper.

[22] Given the number of vacant jobs and the number of unemployed for the entire nation, the smaller of the two figures (or either one if they are equal) may be taken as a rough indication of the size of the structural problem.

[23] The new annual report on manpower (see n. 3) should foster a more balanced approach to the problem of unemployment. This report is required by the Manpower Development and Training Act of 1962.

FRITZ MACHLUP

International Economic Co-operation

THE subject of my paper could be dealt with in a variety of ways. For example, I might choose a *historical* approach, starting with whatever international economic arrangements could be found in the ancient world, proceeding to the best-known international agreements about commerce in the Middle Ages, and expatiating on the broader scope of international economic co-operation in the nineteenth century, before arriving at the story of the multiplication of international economic organizations in the twentieth century, particularly since 1945.

Alternatively, I might choose a *theoretical* approach, discussing the abstract principles which aid in the analysis of the international movements of persons, goods, services, funds, and ideas and, thus, in the understanding of the economic effects of measures hindering or facilitating these movements. The significance of such an approach can be shown by pointing to the fact that many, perhaps most, of the existing intergovernmental agreements and organizations for international economic co-operation are largely designed to undo or alleviate the effects of unco-operative national measures which restrict the international movements of persons, goods, and funds. An analysis of the net effects requires the use of theoretical constructs and models.

Another approach would be an *institutional* one; at its core would be an enumeration and description of all agreements, organizations, associations, agencies, practices, and measures for international economic co-operation; and it would include discussions of the political and social forces leading to their establishment and the legal forms in which they appear and operate.

A *policy* approach to our subject would include both institutional aspects and theoretical techniques plus a discussion of the partly con-

FRITZ MACHLUP is Walker Professor of Economics and International Finance at Princeton University.

flicting objectives pursued by governments and various national and supranational interest groups.

A *taxonomic* approach would concentrate on various distinctions and classifications in order to group different types and form of institutions in some meaningful way. The distinctions might be according to geographic area, number or type of parties involved, economic activity concerned, legal forms employed, objectives pursued, and so forth.

I have decided against a consistent use of any of these approaches and to serve, instead, a menu containing something of everything. There will be a historical sketch, to begin with. The institutional offering will be an enumeration of intergovernmental organizations and a discussion of the other types of existing institutions for international economic co-operation. The taxonomic ingredient will consist of classifications according to various principles. Theoretical analysis will be mixed in at many points—for this is necessary if we are to make any sense of the whole thing—but it will remain as inconspicuous as possible. And there will be some admixture of policy implications, enough for pragmatists to find the fare comestible. Our general dietary rule will be to offer small helpings of each course so that we may end up wishing for a bit more of everything.

History

Let us first embark on an excursion back to the records of the earliest times. Historical sight-seeing saves us from myopic concentration on the present-day situation and may give us a broader understanding of some of the issues involved. Regarding the subject before us, though, the glimpses into early history may chiefly confirm us in the usual prejudice that the world has changed so much that the present can receive little illumination from a searchlight directed at the distant past.

One may even question whether the phrase "international economic co-operation" makes much sense in a discussion of ancient or medieval history. "International" is a word coined in 1780 by Jeremy Bentham; "economic" as an adjective has gained wide currency only since 1830; only "co-operation" is a much older word, but precisely this may least apply to the early stages of history. When two ancient or medieval states or cities agreed to co-operate it was almost regularly at the expense of a third, and though this kind of co-operation is far from unknown in our time and is perhaps most common in the policies of common markets, it is not quite what an idealist is inclined to expect from co-operation.

Searching the pages of history, we find economic co-operation among states chiefly in matters of coinage, trade privileges for merchants, shipping and land transportation, and the joint exercise of monopoly controls over agricultural or mineral products. Almost all of these instances of co-operation were bilateral, not multilateral; exceptions can be found in intergovernmental commodity agreements —cartels for the joint exploitation of consumers.

Any selection for presentation here is necessarily arbitrary. First place should perhaps be given to the First Treaty between Rome and Carthage. The terms of this treaty, which divided spheres of commercial interests and trading territories—Libya, Sardinia, Sicily, *et al.*— were engraved on a bronze tablet. The time of this treaty, according to Polybius' account, was set as 508–507 B.C., but this has remained a controversial question among historians. The Second Treaty between Rome and Carthage, in 348 B.C., again provided for a division of territories for trade and for the mutual guaranty of harbor privileges.[1]

Just for color, we might mention another treaty of the same period but between different parties: a commercial treaty between Athens and the Satrap Orontes of Mysia, *ca.* 349–348 B.C. Fragments of a marble stele are the documentary evidence of this historical fact.[2] Different in theme is a "monetary pact" between Mytilene and Phocaea, probably between 400 and 394 B.C., which was found inscribed on a stele of gray marble. It provided for the issue of gold coins by the two cities—each to exercise this right in alternate years— and for severe penalties against debasement.[3]

It is not entirely arbitrary, but more a matter of the way history has presented itself, if we now jump almost fifteen hundred years to the next example suitable for our selection, a treaty between Pisa and Lucca in 1181 A.D. By this covenant the two republics agreed to divide on a fifty-fifty basis their profits from coinage, the net revenues from port fees, the net earnings from both republics' salt monopolies and from Pisa's monopoly in iron and iron ore, and finally the revenue from Pisa's seaport customhouse.[4]

The twelfth and thirteenth centuries yield a good many examples of commercial treaties. For instance, several Italian commercial colonies obtained all sorts of privileges in the Holy Land; in the Convention of Nymphaeum in 1261, the Republic of Genoa and Emperor

---

[1] Hermann Bengtson (ed.), *Die Staatsverträge des Altertums* (Munich and Berlin: C. H. Beck, 1962), pp. 16–20, 306–9.

[2] *Op. cit.*, pp. 303–5.

[3] Marcus N. Tod (ed.), *A Selection of Greek Historical Inscriptions* (Oxford: Clarendon Press, 1948), II, 34–36.

[4] Jakob Strieder, *Studien zur Geschichte kapitalistischer Organisationsformen* (Munich and Leipzig: Duncker & Humblot, 1914), p. 163.

Michael Palaeologus of the Byzantine Empire exchanged trading rights and exemption from duties for their merchants; this agreement was expanded in 1267. A year later a treaty between the Doge of Venice and the Byzantine Emperor gave similar trading privileges to Venetian merchants, although in 1261 the Genoese had been promised exclusion of their rivals, except the Pisans, from the Byzantine trade; and in 1277 this Venetian-Byzantine treaty was expanded in scope as well as territory.[5]

An intergovernmental cartel agreement was negotiated, according to documents dating from 1301, between the King of Naples, as an owner of saltworks, with the royal French saltworks at Aigues-Mortes. The two royal courts were the parties to the agreed *"societas communis venditionis,"* joint sales syndicate, designed to increase the fiscal revenues for both; the agreement was to be binding on the tenants operating the saltworks.[6]

In our survey, a sure place must be given to the Hanseatic League, which had a widespread network of loose agreements among private traders, towns, cities, states, kings, and even the High Master of the Teutonic Order and operated for several centuries in several countries, chiefly England, Holland, Scandinavia, Russia, and Germany. As one historian said, "Its foundation was no doubt facilitated by the mediaeval affinity for co-operative action and for monopoly."[7]

To mention only a few milestones in the history of the League: in 1252, German merchants received a special grant of privileges from the city of Bruges, in Flanders; in the Carta Mercatoria of 1303, King Edward I gave certain exclusive rights to German merchants trading in England; in 1367, the representatives of seventy-seven towns from various lands concluded the Confederation of Cologne; in the Peace of Stralsund of 1370, the League, having defeated King Waldemar IV of Denmark, secured its control over the Baltic trade and also over Scandinavian politics, since it could veto succession to the Danish throne if the candidate was unwilling to assure the continuation of the League monopolies; in 1377, Richard II renewed the privileges of the League in England; after a conflict with England, the Treaty of Utrecht, in 1474, left the League in full possession of its privileges (which were to last until the days of Queen Elizabeth); but in 1494, Tsar Ivan III drove the German merchants from Novgorod and

---

[5] Deno John Geanakoplos, *Emperor Michael Palaeologus and the West* (Cambridge, Mass.: Harvard University Press, 1959), pp. 87 ff., 206 ff., 214 ff., 301 ff.

[6] Adolf Schaube, *Handelsgeschichte der romanischen Völker des Mittelmeergebietes bis zum Ende der Kreuzzüge* (Munich and Berlin: R. Oldenbourg, 1906), pp. 650–51.

[7] William L. Langer (ed.), *An Encyclopedia of World History* (Boston: Houghton-Mifflin Co., 1940), p. 312.

closed the Hanseatic *Kontor* which they had maintained for three hundred years as the eastern terminus of their trade route and as the center of their Russian trade; in 1629, the assembly of the weakened League entrusted the guardianship of the common welfare to Lübeck, Hamburg, and Bremen; in 1669, the last assembly was held, though League *Kontors* survived in Bergen until 1775, in London until 1852, and in Augsburg until 1863. So rough an outline of the story of the Hanseatic League cannot possibly do justice to this remarkable institution, which may qualify for the designation of a really international organization for international economic co-operation and which is unique in several respects, of which its longevity is not the least.[8]

A fine example of an international cartel involving several governments is provided by the alum agreement, which was first concluded in 1470 between Pope Paul II and King Ferrante of Naples. It provided for co-operative pricing and selling of alum from the Papal mines in Tolfa, operated by the Medicis under contract with the Apostolic Chamber, and from the Neapolitan mines in Ischia. All orders and shipments were divided fifty-fifty, except for sales to certain destinations (Bruges and Venice), for which fixed quotas were reserved to the Papal mines. To avoid competition from Turkish alum, the Pope agreed to administer annual admonitions to all Christendom against trade in the Turkish product; in addition, all ships carrying Turkish alum were subject to seizure. Some of the collateral agreements of the cartel and of its two partners are highly interesting; for example, exclusive sales-agency contracts were concluded between the Apostolic Chamber and a Venetian merchant, though there were also direct sales to the Republic of Venice; a Papal Nuntius negotiated with King Edward IV about English import prohibitions for alum from competing sources; a contract was made with Duke Charles the Bold of Burgundy, providing for the prohibition of imports of non-Roman alum and for clerical as well as secular sanctions against offenders. The international co-operation in the sale of high-priced alum lasted for at least a century, largely because any competition emerging from newly discovered sources was soon regulated, thanks to the skill of a large trading company in Antwerp which had been given trading privileges by Duke Philip the Handsome and Emperor Maximilian I.[9]

The tradition of bilateral commercial treaties between countries continued throughout the centuries. For example, in a treaty between

[8] *Ibid.*, pp. 204–5, 216, 306, 312, 314–15. Michael Postan and E. E. Rich (eds.), *The Cambridge Economic History of Europe,* II (Cambridge: Cambridge University Press, 1952), 223–32.

[9] See Strieder, *op. cit.,* pp. 168–83.

England and the Netherlands in 1496, called the *Intercursus Magnus*, the contracting parties granted mutual privileges to the English and the Flemings and agreed to fixed duties. Skipping a couple of centuries, we may mention a commercial treaty between England and France, in 1713, which gained special significance later when it served John Adams as a pattern for his Model Treaty and, finally, the Treaty of Amity and Commerce between France and the United States, in 1785, the first commercial treaty of this country.[10]

In the nineteenth century, probably the most important development in international economic co-operation was the *German Zollverein*, the customs union of the many separated German states, whose trade had been seriously hampered by their separate tariffs. This customs union, initiated by Prussia when she established a uniform tariff for all her territories in 1819, was concluded in 1833 and broadened in 1853 and 1867. The *Zollverein* is the prize example of the possibility of economic integration leading eventually to political union.

Our brief historical survey has been of "economic co-operation" in an admittedly peculiar sense, perhaps not acceptable to many. Yet, from the very beginning, co-operation in economic matters has meant combination to exclude others, to protect vested interests, and to restrain competition; only rarely has it meant working with others to help many at the expense of none. Perhaps we are witnessing now a real change in attitude. When John Adams reviewed the illiberal way in which France interpreted the presumably liberal Treaty of Amity and Commerce, he expressed doubt that "the things signified" by the "unpopular" words "monopoly, prohibition, exclusion, and navigation acts . . . will be abolished so soon as some speculators imagine."[11] This was almost one hundred and eighty years ago. Have we progressed much since then? The present discussion will perhaps provide some clues for an answer.

TAXONOMY

A bit of taxonomy is needed even before we go on, especially before we proceed to a survey of existing institutions; otherwise we would not know what to survey. We know only that we are interested in instruments of international co-operation: they may be creations of governments, of private associations, or of individuals and

10 Felix Gilbert, *To the Farewell Address: Ideas of Early American Foreign Policy* (Princeton, N.J.: Princeton University Press, 1961), pp. 50, 84.

11 Letter from John Adams to John Jay, August 29, 1785, in *The Diplomatic Correspondence of the United States of America* (Washington: Francis Preston Blair, 1833), IV, 339.

firms; they may be conventions, treaties, agreements, contracts, or informal arrangements; they may be organizations or joint agencies, temporary or permanent, with closed membership or open; they may be departments or agencies of individual national governments; they may consist of laws, regulations, policies, or particular measures and actions. A tabulation of all these possible instruments of international co-operation can show a vast number of combinations—and therefore the impossibility of a quick and complete survey (see Table 1).

TABLE 1

INSTRUMENTS OF INTERNATIONAL CO-OPERATION

Governments	Private Associations	Individuals and Corporations
Conventions, treaties, agreements, arrangements among governments of different countries, bilateral or multilateral	Agreements, arrangements among associations operating in different countries	Contracts, agreements, arrangements among firms operating in different countries
Intergovernmental organizations, temporary or permanent, closed membership or open	International non-governmental organizations	Joint agencies of firms residing in different countries
National government departments and agencies for foreign affairs	National (private) organizations for foreign affairs	Individuals and corporations within a country operating for the benefit of foreign countries
National laws and regulations for the benefit of foreign countries		
Government policies and actions for the benefit of foreign countries	Association policies and actions for the benefit of foreign countries	Private business policies and actions for the benefit of foreign countries

Other distinctions must be made and will be made later. By now, however, we are convinced that no survey presented within the scope of an essay could possibly cover the whole gamut. It would be too big a task if co-operation among private business firms in different countries were to be included, let alone co-operation among firms in the same country regarding their trade with foreign countries. Lest someone think that such policies would not belong to our subject, let us recall the "voluntary" quota restrictions which Japanese textile producers had to impose upon themselves in exporting to the United States, in order to co-operate with the U.S. government, under the threat of higher U.S. import duties or import quotas for the protection of poor textile manufacturers in the United States. Does this not qualify as international economic co-operation? Even if we shall not deal with them, let us not forget these private and semiprivate business agreements, including the hundreds of private international cartel agreements under which industrialists in different countries co-operate with one another in reducing competition in international trade.

INSTITUTIONS

Let us leave to one side the conventions, treaties, agreements, etc., and concentrate first on permanent international organizations and later on national agencies for international economic co-operation.

INTERNATIONAL ORGANIZATIONS

In order to obtain an idea of the number of international organizations, we may turn to the *Yearbook of International Organizations*, published biennially by the Union of International Associations, formed in 1907. The increase in entries is remarkable: the 1958–59 edition listed 1,209 international organizations; the 1960–61 edition, 1,420; and the 1962–63 edition lists 1,710 (plus some national organizations in "consultative" status with the United Nations). Included are only organizations currently in existence. If defunct agencies were included, the number since the Congress of Vienna, in 1815, would exceed 2,000.

Of the 1,710 organizations listed in 1962–63, 170 are intergovernmental organizations (IGO's); 1,324 are international non-governmental organizations (NGO's); and 216 are "non-governmental groupings in the European Community." The IGO's include no bilateral organizations; that is, a minimum of three governments have to be members. The NGO's include only registered organizations; informal associations and those registered only nationally are not included. Less than one-third of the IGO's serve chiefly political, military, scientific, medical, sanitary, educational, social, or juridical purposes, while over two-thirds are instruments of international economic co-operation.

A compilation of 125 economic IGO's is given in Table 2.[12] The arrangement of the table can be briefly explained. The first group, with 25 entries, consists of the "UN family," that is, the permanent economic committees of the United Nations, the specialized agencies, and other permanent bodies closely related to the United Nations. The second group, the other economic IGO's, is divided into six subgroups according to geographic reference: "world-wide" are organi-

---

12 *The Yearbook of International Organizations* (Brussels, 1963) was used as the chief but not sole source for this information. A few organizations listed in Table 2 are not yet included in the *Yearbook,* and for some entries more recent information has become available.

TABLE 2

INTERGOVERNMENTAL ORGANIZATIONS FOR ECONOMIC CO-OPERATION

FULL TITLE IN ENGLISH	ABBREVIATIONS:		YEAR ESTAB-LISHED	No. OF MEMBER GOVTS.*
	English	French or Other		

United Nations Committees, Specialized Agencies, and Other Bodies Closely Related to the UN

FULL TITLE IN ENGLISH	English	French or Other	YEAR	No.
Economic and Social Council	ECOSOC		1945	111
Economic Commission for Europe	ECE	CEE	1945	UN
Economic Commission for Asia and the Far East	ECAFE	CEAEO	1945	UN
Economic Commission for Latin America	ECLA	CEAL	1945	UN
Economic Commission for Africa	ECA	CEA	1945	UN
Technical Assistance Board	TAB	BAT	1949	UN
Permanent Central Opium Board	PCOB	CCPO	1928	UN
Drug Supervisory Body	DSP	OCS	1933	UN
United Nations Children's Fund	UNICEF	FISE	1946	UN
Office of the UN High Commissioner for Refugees	UNHCR	HCNUR	1951	UN
United Nations Special Fund			1959	UN
International Telecommunication Union	ITU	UIT	1865	113
International Radio Consultative Committee		CCIR	1927	ITU
International Frequency Registration Board	IFRB	BIRF	1947	ITU
International Telegraph and Telephone Consultative Committee		CCITT	1957	ITU
Universal Postal Union	UPU	UPU	1874	115
International Labor Organization	ILO	OIT	1919	104
Food and Agriculture Organization of the UN	FAO	OAA	1945	104
International Civil Aviation Organization	ICAO	OACI	1945	98
International Monetary Fund	IMF	FMI	1945	102
International Bank for Reconstruction and Development	IBRD	BIRD	1945	101
International Finance Corporation	IFC	SFI	1956	75
International Development Association	IDA	AID	1959	86
General Agreement on Tariffs and Trade	GATT		1948	50
International Atomic Energy Agency	IAEA	AIEA	1956	77
Intergovernmental Maritime Consultative Organization	IMCO	OMCI	1959	51

Other Intergovernmental Economic Organizations

FULL TITLE IN ENGLISH	English	French or Other	YEAR	No.
World-wide:				
International Bureau of Weights and Measures		BIPM	1875	38
International Union for the Protection of Industrial Property		UIPPI	1883	49
International Union for the Protection of Literary and Artistic Works		UIPOLA	1886	45
United International Bureaux for Protection of Industrial Literary and Artistic Property		BIRPI	1888	49

* As of 1962. In some instances it was possible to adjust numbers to the status of September, 1963.

TABLE 2—*Continued*

Full Title in English	Abbreviations:		Year Estab-lished	No. of Member Govts.*
	English	French or Other		

Other Intergovernmental Economic Organizations—*Continued*

World-wide—Continued

International Patent Institute.........		IIB	1947	9
Intergovernmental Copyright Committee	IGCC	CIDA	1952	12
International Union for the Publication of Custom Tariffs..................			1891	66
Customs Co-operation Council........	CCC	CCD	1950	28
International Relief Union............	IRU	UIS	1927	22
International Exhibition Bureau.......		BIE	1931	29
International Vine and Wine Office....	IWO	OIV	1924	22
International Tea Committee.........			1933	8
International Commisssion for Agri-cultural Industries.................		CIIA	1934	41
International Cotton Advisory Com-mittee............................	ICAC	CCIC	1939	35
Internationl Rubber Study Group.....	IRSG		1944	24
International Whaling Commission.....	IWC	CIB	1946	17
International Wool Study Group......	IWSG		1947	35
International Poplar Commission......	IPC	CIP	1947	12
International Rice Commission........	IRC	CIR	1948	27
International Wheat Council.........			1949	44
International Chestnut Commission....		CIC	1951	9
International Sugar Council...........			1953	42
International Olive Oil Council.......			1955	10
International Tin Council.............			1956	20
International Coffee Study Group.....			1958	33
International Lead and Zinc Study Group..........................			1959	25
Organization of Petroleum Exporting Countries.......................	OPEC	OPEP	1960	8

Intercontinental:

Postal Union of the Americas and Spain	PUAS	UPAE	1911	23
Arab Postal Union..................	APU	UPA	1954	12
Commonwealth Economic Committee..	CEC		1925	12
Commonwealth Agricultural Bureaux..	CAB		1929	12
Commonwealth Telecommunications Board.........................			1949	9
Colombo Plan Council for Technical Co-operation in South and South-East Asia......................			1950	19
Bank for International Settlements.....	BIS	BRI	1930	26
Inter-Allied Reparations Agency.......	IARA		1946	19
Tripartite Commission for the Restitu-tion of Monetary Gold.............			1946	3
Arab Development Bank (not yet op-erating).........................		BAD	1957	9
Organization for Economic Co-opera-tion and Development.............	OECD	OCDE	1961	20
Development Assistance Committee....	DAC		1961	12
Central Banks Gold Pool............			1962	8
South Pacific Commission............			1947	6
Indo-Pacific Fisheries Council.........	IPFC	CIPP	1948	17
International Commission for the Northwest Atlantic Fisheries.......	ICNAF		1950	12

TABLE 2—*Continued*

| FULL TITLE IN ENGLISH | ABBREVIATIONS: | | YEAR ESTAB- LISHED | No. OF MEMBER GOVTS.* |
	English	French or Other		
		Other Intergovernmental Economic Organizations—*Continued*		
Intercontinental—Continued				
European and Mediterranean Plant Protection Organization...........	EPPO	OEPP	1951	31
General Fisheries Council for the Mediterranean......................	GFCM	CGPM	1952	13
Permanent Commission for the Conservation of the Maritime Resources of the South Pacific...............		[CPPS]	1952	3
International North Pacific Fisheries Commission.....................	INPFC		1952	3
Near East Forestry Commission.......	NEFC	CFPO	1953	16
North Pacific Fur Seal Commission....			1958	4
Council for Mutual Economic Aid (Moscow)	CMEA	CAEM [or Comecon]	1949	9
Organization for the Collaboration of Railways (Warsaw)...............		[OSShD]	1956	12
Intergovernmental Committee for European Migration.................	ICEM	CIME	1951	30
European:				
Central Commission for the Navigation of the Rhine....................		CCR	1815	7
Administrative Center of Social Security for Rhine Boatmen.............			1950	5
Central Office for International Railway Transport...................		OCTI	1890	25
European Conference of Ministers of Transport......................	ECMT	CEMT	1953	17
European Company for the Financing of Railway Rolling Stock..........		Eurofima	1955	16
European Conference of Postal and Telecommunications Administrations.		CEPT	1959	19
Permanent Commission of the International Fisheries Convention........			1946	14
European Forestry Commission.......,	EFC	CEF	1948	22
Danube Commission...............		CD	1948	7
International Moselle Company.......		SIM	1957	3
European Coal and Steel Community..	ECSC	CECA	1952	6
European Productivity Agency........	EPA	AEP	1953	18
European Nuclear Energy Agency.....	ENEA		1957	18
European Atomic Energy Community..	Euratom	CEEA	1958	6
Benelux Economic Union.............		Benelux	1958	3
European Economic Community.......	EEC	CEE	1958	6
Economic and Social Committee.......	ECSC		1958	6
European Investment Bank...........	EIB	BEI	1958	6
European Monetary Agreement.......	EMA	AME	1958	11
European Free Trade Association......	EFTA	AELE	1960	7
Scandinavian Patent Committee.......			1955	4
European Company for the Chemical Processing of Irradiated Fuels.......		Eurochemie	1959	13
Union for the Protection of New Varieties of Plants...................			1961	8

TABLE 2—*Continued*

FULL TITLE IN ENGLISH	ABBREVIATIONS:		YEAR ESTAB- LISHED	No. OF MEMBER GOVTS.*
	English	French or Other		

Other Intergovernmental Economic Organizations—*Continued*

FULL TITLE IN ENGLISH	English	French or Other	YEAR ESTAB- LISHED	No. OF MEMBER GOVTS.*
American:				
Inter-American Radio Office..........		OIR	1937	12
Inter-American Conference on Social Security........................		CISS	1942	20
Latin-American Forestry Commission..	LAFC	CFLA	1948	24
Latin-American Centre for Monetary Studies........................		CEMLA	1949	15
Central-American Research Institute for Industry......................		ICAITI	1956	6
Inter-American Nuclear Energy Commission........................	IANEL	CIEN	1959	21
Inter-American Development Bank....	IDB	BID	1959	20
Central-American Common Market....	CACM		1960	5
Permanent Secretariat for Central-American Economic Integration.....		SIECA	1960	
Central-American Bank for Economic Integration.....................	CABEI	BCIE	1961	5
Central-American Clearing House......		CCCA	1961	5
Latin-American Free Trade Association.	LAFTA	ALALE	1961	9
Inter-American Committee for Agricultural Development.............		CIDA	1961	21
Latin-American Institute for Economic and Social Planning...............			1962	8
Alliance for Progress................			1962	20
Asian:				
Asian Productivity Organization.......	APO		1961	8
African:				
African Postal and Telecommunications Union..........................	APTU		1935	13
African Telecommunication Union		UAT	1961	6
Interafrican Bureau for Soils and Rural Economy........................		BIS	1950	6
Commission for Technical Co-operation in Africa South of the Sahara.......		CCTA	1950	22
Inter-African Labour Institute........		IIT	1953	8
Inter-African Committee on Statistics..		CIE	1954	8
East African Common Services Organization........................	EACSO		1962	3
African Development Bank..........			1962	9
West African Monetary Union........			1962	7

zations with member governments on more than two continents; "intercontinental" are those with members on two continents or confined to circumscribed groupings of nations, such as the British Commonwealth or those bordering the Mediterranean or the Pacific Ocean; the others are European, American, Asian, and African. (Note that it is not by mistake that the Intergovernmental Committee for European Migration [ICEM] is listed as intercontinental, for it includes African and Asian members.)

The order in which the organizations are listed combines, somewhat uneasily, two different principles: it is partly chronological, partly functional. This may look disorderly, but there is some sense to it. For example, on the list of world-wide IGO's, the Union Internationale pour la Protection de la Propriété Industrielle (UIPPI) appears as the second entry because it was established in 1883; it is immediately followed by all the other organizations concerned with patents, trade marks, and copyrights, although some, such as the IIB and IGCC, were established much later. The last entry in this cluster, with a 1952 date, is then followed by one with an 1891 date, dealing with import duties.

While we are on the subject of dates, we may indulge in a little historical curiosity and take note of the age of some of our organizations. The oldest of them is the Central Commission for the Navigation of the Rhine (CCR), established at the Congress of Vienna in 1815. It will soon have its one hundred and fiftieth anniversary. The two that come next in age are now part of the United Nations family; they are the International Telecommunication Union (ITU), which goes back, though under a different name, to the International Telegraph Convention of 1865, and the Universal Postal Union (UPU), which was established in 1874. Altogether eight of the economic IGO's operating today were set up in the nineteenth century.

Two very important European IGO's are not in Table 2, because they have ceased operations. The Organization for European Economic Co-operation (OEEC), established in 1948, was superseded in 1960 by the Organization for Economic Co-operation and Development (OECD); and the European Payments Union (EPU), set up in 1950, was liquidated when most European currencies had become convertible in 1958 and these regional payments arrangements had thus become unnecessary.

The number of members varies, of course, with the scope and function of the organization. The Benelux Economic Union (Benelux) is by definition confined to 3 member governments, and the Central American organizations, with only 4 members at first and 5 now, cannot increase membership to more than 6, the number of Central

American states. The world-wide IGO's outside the UN family have up to 66 members. The UN had 110 members in December, 1962; and the UPU had 114; both increase as more independent states come into existence.

A classification by economic function depends on the classifier's taxonomic taste. I propose to focus on the object of international economic activity with which the particular intergovernmental organization is primarily concerned; this may be movements across national borders of persons, goods, services, funds, or ideas. Where one cannot single out one of these as the chief concern, other distinguishing labels must be provided. The 125 IGO's on our lists can be classified as follows: 2 concern themselves primarily with the international movement of persons, that is, with migration; 26, with the movement of goods, that is, with international trade, tariffs, and particular commodity problems; 26 are concerned primarily with service industries such as transportation, communication, and atomic energy; 20 are chiefly concerned with the movement of funds, that is, international payments, loans, or grants; 29 organizations serve specialized functions, for example, they seek the harmonization of national legislation and policies regarding labor, agriculture, forestry, fisheries, industrial property, etc.; and the remaining 22 organizations may be grouped with a label of "general" or "miscellaneous," because they deal with more general problems, with a combination of problems, or with matters, such as technical aid, which do not fit into the other classes.

We shall not attempt a similar compilation and survey of NGO's for economic co-operation. It would take too much time and would not provide much intellectual stimulation. Suffice it to say that the 1962–63 *Yearbook* lists 497 NGO's with economic functions, apart from the non-governmental groupings in the European Community. To mention only a few: the International Chamber of Commerce, the International Confederation of Free Trade Unions, the International Clearing Union, the International Union of Marine Insurance, and a good many international labor organizations and trade associations. Some of the "non-governmental" organizations are really semigovernmental in that many of their members are corporations owned or controlled by governments. The International Air Transport Association (IATA), comprising 93 airlines from 71 nations, is a case in point, inasmuch as most of the airlines—practically all but the American—are government-owned. The IATA serves international co-operation chiefly in the sense in which a cartel is of service to its members and of disservice to consumers, by substituting co-operative price-fixing and price maintenance for price competition—with the result that the airlines, barred from competing through lower fares, are confined to competing largely through extravagant advertising.

Special mention may be made of a recent arrival on the scene, the Union of the Industries of the European Economic Community (UNICE). This is one of the 216 non-governmental groups in the European Economic Community (EEC); the others are essentially the Common Market trade associations of individual industries and trades in the six EEC countries, covering products from aerated drinks to margarine, powdered milk, sewing machines, ice cream, mayonnaise, sugar, sugar beets, ceramic tiles, glassware, watches, fruit juices, wines, milk, textiles, clothing, footwear, hides, fuel, metal scrap, wastepaper, and macaroni. These 216 Common Market NGO's are apart from the approximately 500 other registered NGO's operating in the area of international economic co-operation.

NATIONAL AGENCIES FOR INTERNATIONAL CO-OPERATION

In order to deal effectively with problems of international economic co-operation, national governments have set up their own agencies. These are institutions unilaterally established chiefly or solely for the purpose of international economic co-operation. By mentioning some of the agencies of the U.S. government we may gain an impression of the nature and significance of this type of institution. There is the Export-Import Bank (EXIMbank) of Washington and the Agency for International Development (AID)—the two chief agencies for channeling government funds to foreign borrowers and grantees. The latter has had an interesting political history because, in order to mollify the temper of an unsympathetic Congress, the name of this agency has been changed several times. It started as ECA, became MSA, then FOA, later ICA, more recently DLF, and is now AID. Apparently, like a criminal, it has had to use several aliases. Other agencies deal with international problems of agriculture, labor, commerce, etc. The St. Lawrence Seaway Development Corporation should perhaps be given a prominent place, because the joint exploitation of natural resources by neighboring countries is an important task of economic co-operation.

Lest we forget the role which non-governmental national organizations play in international economic co-operation, let us name a few of them: the Committee for a National Trade Policy (CNTP), a businessmen's association for the promotion of international trade; the Society for International Development (SID) and the Committee for International Economic Growth (CIEG), two organizations to encourage U.S. aid for less-developed nations; the Foreign Credit Insurance Association (FCIA), a group of over seventy private insurance companies in partnership with the EXIMbank. We know of no attempt to count the number of private organizations of this kind in the United States or elsewhere.

To continue this largely enumerative institutional survey might become increasingly dull. Let us therefore vary the approach and explore, somewhat more systematically, the policy implications of international economic co-operation. This presupposes a theoretical analysis of the objectives sought, methods employed, and effects achieved; but we shall avoid being ostentatious about the theorizing involved.

POLICIES

In a casual observation we said before that many of the inter-governmental agreements and organizations for international economic co-operation were designed largely to undo or alleviate the restrictive effects of unco-operative national measures. To show that this was not a wild exaggeration, some examples shall be provided here.

Nations, without exception, employ import duties and other trade barriers to restrict the international movement of goods; international co-operation is then instituted to lower the national barriers, or often only to check their further elevation, or at the very least to help traders obtain reliable information about the barriers which national governments have erected. The General Agreement on Tariffs and Trade (GATT) tries to lower the barriers; the Customs Cooperation Council (CCC), the European Economic Community, and the European Free Trade Association (EFTA) have the first two tasks—lowering barriers or checking their further increase—though the EEC has been found raising some external tariffs while reducing internal tariffs. The third task, supplying information about the tariffs adopted, is performed by the International Union for the Publication of Custom Tariffs. None of these instruments of international co-operation would be needed were it not for national unco-operativeness in matters of international trade.

A similar statement may be made with regard to international payments. If all countries had subordinated their national economic goals to principles of international co-ordination and observed the orthodox rules of the gold-standard game without any restriction on foreign payments, no special agencies and international organizations in the monetary field would have been necessary. The International Monetary Fund (IMF), the European Payments Union, the European Monetary Agreement (EMA), and the Central American Clearing House (CCCA), are some of the organizations, past or present, designed to cope with problems arising from currency inconvertibility under foreign-exchange restrictions or from exchange-rate disalignment under self-centered monetary policies.

We must not, however, overplay this theme. There exist international arrangements for economic co-operation which are not merely to offset unco-operative national policies. As examples let us mention the organizations to promote transportation and communication, the agreements to help producer interests in primary commodities, and the schemes to assist less-developed countries through technical as well as financial aid. (Several of these countries, though, might be aided more effectively by an abolition of all trade barriers by the industrial nations.)

THE MOVEMENT OF PERSONS

With regard to the international movement of persons—emigration and immigration—it is difficult to say whether the international co-operation of recent years is merely a relaxation of the isolationist policies of nations or rather a positive program to redistribute people to areas of higher productivity. The judgment will depend on whether one regards restriction on immigration as unco-operative or rather as something "natural." In any case, the change in attitudes in these matters that has occurred in Europe since World War II is remarkable. There used to be the feeling that, if a nation permitted immigration on a large scale, it would import unemployment or depress wages. Now the fastest growing countries have opened the gates to floods of foreign labor, and it seems that exactly this has given impetus to economic growth. The greater the number of workers received from abroad, the higher rose the employment rate; that is, the labor force increased, but employment increased even faster. To make it absolutely clear: the number of jobs increased faster than the number of foreign laborers arriving in the particular countries. Needless to say, the reference here is to western Europe, not the United States, where the attitude regarding immigration has remained unco-operative, narrow-minded, and race-conscious, except for some emergency actions in particular years (such as after the 1956 flight of Hungarian refugees).

Statistical figures may illustrate the issue under discussion. The resettlement in Western Germany of refugees from the eastern provinces of prewar Germany, from Soviet-dominated middle Germany (now East Germany), and from foreign countries, mainly in eastern Europe, was one of the largest migrations in modern Europe. Almost 7 million persons whose homes at the outbreak of World War II had been in these areas were resettled in the West Zone of Germany by

October, 1946. By October, 1951, the total had risen to 9.8 million, 22.6 per cent of the 1946 population of what is now the Federal Republic of Germany. These new arrivals accounted for 67.6 per cent of the total increase in the population of Western Germany between 1946 and 1951.[13] The boost in the German labor force was associated not with unemployment but with over-full employment. And in the late 1950's large numbers of foreign workers, mostly Italians, were brought to Germany under various recruitment plans.[14]

The comparative figures for other European countries are also remarkable. For example, in France the number of work permits issued to first-time applicants—three-fifths of whom were seasonal foreign labor—between 1950 and 1960 amounted to 23.8 per cent of the French population growth in this ten-year period.[15] For the United Kingdom, the immigration statistics are extraordinary: between 1946 and 1957, gross immigration from all parts of the world was 1.5 million persons, while total population increased by only 1.9 million, so that immigration accounted for about 78.6 per cent of the population increase. The explanation lies in the simultaneous emigration from the United Kingdom, which actually exceeded the immigration.[16]

Switzerland, too, has in recent years received foreign workers on a large scale. Between 1959 and 1961 over a million work permits were issued, which is 3.6 times the natural population increase of the two years, or 19.1 per cent of the entire 1960 population of Switzerland.[17] All these permits, however, are for temporary stay only; they are for seasonal workers, non-seasonal workers, or frontier commuters. The number of "permanent residence permits" is relatively small. In any case, in August, 1962, Switzerland, with a *de jure* population of about 5.6 million, had some 750,000 foreign workers, amounting to 30 per cent of her total employed labor force.[18] This

[13] *Statistisches Jahrbuch für die Deutsche Bundesrepublik, 1952* (Stuttgart and Cologne: Statistisches Bundesamt, 1952), p. 30.

[14] Heinrich M. Dreyer, "Immigration of Foreign Workers into the Federal Republic of Germany," *International Labour Review*, LXXXIV (July–August, 1961), 1–25.

[15] For the relevant migration figures, see "Immigration in France, 1950–1960," *Migration*, I (July–September, 1961), 60–63. The population figures, unless specifically cited, have been drawn from the United Nations, *Demographic Yearbook, 1961* (New York, 1962), pp. 134–36.

[16] International Labour Office, *International Migration, 1945–1957* (Geneva: 1959), pp. 139–42, 169–73.

[17] *Statistisches Jahrbuch der Schweiz, 1962* (Basel: Eidgenössisches Statistisches Amt, 1962), pp. 10, 87. The natural population increase, 285,000, is a provisional extrapolation published in the *Demographic Yearbook, 1961*.

[18] Vera Lutz, "Foreign Workers and Domestic Wage Levels: With an Illustration from the Swiss Case," *Banca Nazionale del Lavoro Quarterly Review*, No. 64 (March, 1963), p. 4.

explains why an unnamed authority on the country answered a question regarding the employment rate in Switzerland to the effect that 135 per cent of the Swiss labor force was gainfully employed—using "Swiss" as indicating citizenship.

The United States can offer only a two-year period with a comparable record: in 1956–57, 648,500 immigrants were received, which accounted for 21.1 per cent of the increase in population in the two years. For a longer period, the figures are low. Thus, from 1946 to 1961, gross immigration amounted to 3.75 million persons, which is 8.9 per cent of the increase in population.[19]

The willingness of several countries to receive immigrants or admit foreign workers has been of great significance also for countries suffering from "surplus population." Net emigration from Italy was 255,500 persons in 1958 and 371,600 in 1961. Total net emigration in these four years from 1958 to 1961, was 1.23 million, or about 2.5 per cent of Italy's population in 1958.[20] Emigration from Greece in the five years from 1957 to 1961 was 296,000 persons, or about 3.5 per cent of the Greek population in 1957.[21] On the basis of the figures up to 1959, one source estimated that "emigration absorbs yearly some 25 to 30 per cent of the new active population."[22] Since the emigration figure for 1961 (85,263) was virtually twice that for 1959 (43,683), it appears that emigration has come even closer to draining off the excess population of Greece.

A considerable number of bilateral treaties were concluded since the end of World War II with the express purpose of assisting international migration. No fewer than sixteen such treaties—seven between European countries, two between non-European countries, and seven between European and non-European countries—were listed as having been concluded in the ten years from 1946 to 1955, most of them conforming to outlines drawn up by the International Committee for European Migration and the International Labor Organization (ILO).[23]

The liberalization of the international movement of persons is of greatest importance for both the countries which the migrants leave

[19] U.S. Department of Commerce, *Statistical Abstract of the United States, 1962,* pp. 5, 98. Also, *Statistical Abstract, 1958,* p. 93, and *Statistical Abstract, 1951,* p. 94.

[20] *Demographic Yearbook, 1962.*

[21] For the data for 1957 to 1959, see "Emigration from Greece in 1958 and 1959," *Migration,* I (January–March, 1961), 72–76. For 1960 and 1961, see "Emigration from Greece in 1961," *International Labour Review,* LXXXVI (November, 1962), 488–91.

[22] Sotirios Agapitidis, "Emigration from Greece," *Migration,* I (January–March, 1961), 55–61.

[23] *International Migration, 1945–1957,* pp. 285–89.

and the countries to which they go. Both the unloading and the receiving countries gain from the movement of human resources to places where their productivity is higher. But to quash any undue optimism about genuine "co-operation," we should consider the following comment by an analyst of the liberalization of migration in Europe: ". . . the immigration which has actually taken place to Western European countries is clearly not the result of a deliberate policy, inspired by social motives, of admitting people from the poorer parts of the world to share in the benefits of the better endowments with natural resources, capital and entrepreneurship of the richer parts. What effect has actually been achieved in this direction has not been consciously sought."[24]

THE MOVEMENT OF GOODS

The brief references made above to organized international co-operation in the promotion of freer international movement of goods —the references to GATT, EEC, and EFTA—cannot pass as an adequate treatment of world-trade liberalization in recent years. Moreover, the recent excitement about France's blackballing Britain as an applicant for membership in the European Common Market calls for some discussion of the expectations and frustrations regarding the expansion of EEC. Neither of these topics, the development of world trade and the economic consequences of EEC, can be done justice in this essay, but nevertheless some additional space should be devoted to both.

Beginning with the second topic, we should state that the various appraisals of the European Common Market are so confusing because of unresolved conflicts between political and economic objectives. Even experts holding similar philosophies and theories would often assume very different positions in the discussion about the Common Market because for many of them political considerations outweigh economic considerations, at least in this instance, while others rely mainly on economic arguments. Whether EEC means protection more than trade liberalization, trade diversion more than trade creation, cartelization more than increased competition within the member countries—all these and other issues are regarded by some as relatively unimportant, compared with two achievements in the area of international politics. One is the surrender of certain prerogatives of national sovereignty to supranational authorities—a highly important development on the way to a better world order. The other is the chance of a new and permanent friendship between France and Germany, traditional enemy nations—and this would be of paramount

[24] Lutz, *op. cit.*, p. 5.

significance for a safer world peace. Some economists, however, re-fuse to pass judgments on such political questions. Others try to turn into political experts and declare, in reply to the friendship-and-peace argument, that the likelihood of disagreement in the interpretation and implementation of the Treaty of Rome may put the new friend-ship to excessively severe tests and may thus hold more dangers than safeguards for world peace. Even if these premonitions seem reason-able, let us hope that they will prove to have been unduly pessimistic.

Leaving aside the political consequences of EEC and concentrating solely on economic issues, we must first attempt to see what implica-tions the theory of customs unions holds for the case before us. The EEC conception provides for the gradual reduction and eventual removal of all internal tariffs and for the maintenance and partial increase of an external tariff. This discrimination against imports from non-member countries is liable to cause a good deal of trade diversion in disregard of the law of comparative advantage and thus to lead to an inferior geographic division of labor for all regions concerned. The question is how much *new* trade will be created thanks to the abolition of internal tariffs and whether the benefits from this new trade will more than offset the damages caused by the diversions of trade. Some observers are convinced that there will be a net balance of benefits; as evidence for this position they point to the fact that, since the beginning of the EEC, imports to EEC countries from non-member countries have increased faster than the rate of economic growth of the "Inner Six," and hence very much faster than the growth rate of the EFTA countries.[25] Others reject this evidence; they say that the slower growth of the EFTA countries may be partially explained by the trade diversion through EEC discrimina-tion, and they hypothecate that EEC imports from non-member countries might have grown much faster in the absence of the EEC trade policies.

Incidentally, the fast rate of economic growth in the EEC countries is often attributed to the economic integration induced by the Com-mon Market. Several analysts, however, reject this attribution. Others accept the claim, in part, but deny the role of trade policy as the predominant factor; they hold that the freer movement of persons and of capital funds has been more significant in this respect than the internal liberalization of the movement of goods. How much indus-trial investment was actually induced by the external barriers around

[25] From 1958 to 1961, exports from the rest of the world to EEC countries increased from $20.9 to $30.2 billion, and exports from EFTA countries to EEC countries increased from $3.6 to $4.8 billion. The percentage increases over the three-year period were 45 and 33 per cent, respectively. The data are from GATT, *International Trade, 1961* (Geneva, 1962), Appendix, Table 1.

the Common Market and may have contributed to the economic growth of the EEC countries is also an open question. In any case, fast expansion in a protected area due to a high rate of investment that is malinvestment from a world-wide point of view is not necessarily a recommendation for the trade policy at issue.

French resistance against the accession of the United Kingdom to the Common Market has shown that the intentions of at least one country of the six are more protectionist-restrictionist than liberalizing. The next test in this respect will come with the next round of GATT negotiations, when the United States, the EEC members, and other countries of the free world will try to swap tariff reductions. The Trade Expansion Act which the United States passed in 1962, plus the GATT machinery for lowering trade barriers, could, unless France succeeds in blocking also this effort at trade liberalization, achieve real progress in international co-operation designed to permit a freer flow of goods.

Six of the seven EFTA countries—United Kingdom, Denmark, Norway, Sweden, Switzerland, and Portugal—have decided, for the time being, to postpone further efforts to join the EEC; only Austria is negotiating for associate membership. In the pledged removal of internal tariffs the EFTA countries, like the EEC countries, are ahead of the originally agreed time schedule. The intra-EFTA tariffs on industrial trade have already been reduced by 50 per cent and are to reach zero by the end of 1966; an exception has been made for Norway for a few items on which import duties will be abolished in 1970.

The movement for regional tariff arrangements has spread to the Americas. The Latin American Free Trade Association (LAFTA), established when the Treaty of Montevideo came into effect in May, 1961, had its first, rather modest, round of tariff reductions in 1962. Trade among the nine member countries, according to official reports, increased by 36 per cent during one year.[26] The Central American Common Market (CACM), established in 1960, provides for the immediate removal of tariffs and other barriers on certain commodities originating in member countries, for liberalization of trade in other commodities, and for equalization of external tariffs. Agreement has been reached on 95 per cent of all articles and on completely free trade among the five countries by 1966.[27]

A closer look at the actual development of world trade might be illuminating at this point. World trade has been increasing at a fast rate ever since the end of World War II. In order to avoid the need

[26] Bank of London & South America, *Fortnightly Review* (May 4, 1963), p. 391.

[27] Bank of London & South America, *Fortnightly Review* (April 6, 1963), p. 329.

for separating increases in physical volume from increases in prices, we shall confine ourselves to the period 1953 to 1961, in which prices of goods in foreign trade did not change much. (While, according to UN statistics, the index of prices of manufactured goods increased by 9 per cent during these eight years, the price index for all internationally traded goods fell by 2 per cent.) As we see in Table 3, the value of world exports (exclusive of U.S. military exports) at f.o.b. prices, that is, without the cost of transport from the exporting country, increased from $77.6 billion in 1953 to $131.3 billion in 1961. This is an increase of about 70 per cent. Since the volume of commodity output of the world (excluding the Soviet block) increased

TABLE 3

WORLD EXPORTS AT F.O.B.
PRICES, 1953 TO 1961*

(In Billions of Dollars)

1953.	77.6
1954.	82.3
1955.	90.8
1956.	100.5
1957.	108.8
1958.	104.8
1959.	113.1
1960.	125.9
1961.	131.3

* The General Agreement on Tariffs and Trade, *International Trade 1961* (Geneva, September, 1962), p. 6.

in the same period by only 35 per cent, the increase in the international division of labor is quite conspicuous: commodity trade increased twice as fast as commodity production.[28]

Only a relatively small part of the increase, it should be noted, was attributable to development and growth of non-industrial countries; most of the increase occurred in the trade among industrial countries. To be sure, both exports from and imports into non-industrial areas of the world increased significantly, but their share in world trade declined; that is, the increase in exports and imports in the industrial areas of the world was so much greater that their percentage share in total trade increased. To what extent the increase in world trade can be attributed to policies of trade liberalization—to reductions of tariffs and other trade barriers, including the relaxation of payments restrictions—and to what extent the increase was due to increased opportunities afforded by the wider comparative advantages of international division of labor, cannot be determined. In a sense, however,

[28] *International Trade 1961*, pp. 5–8.

every increase in world trade, and especially an increase at a rate faster than that of the growth of production and income, may be regarded as a widening of the scope of international economic co-operation.

THE MOVEMENT OF FUNDS

We have already referred to organized co-operation for achieving freer movement of funds across national borders and particularly to the co-operative efforts to re-establish currency convertibility after many governments had for several years placed heavy restrictions on foreign payments, both on current account (goods, services, donations) and on capital account (loans, securities, direct investment). The institutions and machineries set up for removing these obstacles to the free flow of funds from country to country were of utmost importance for the economies concerned. Most significant in this area was the EPU, the payments system for seventeen countries from 1950 to 1958. It became superfluous when most of the member countries had removed or suspended their most restrictive exchange regulations and had thus re-established currency convertibility.

Equally important has been economic co-operation through government grants and loans for relief, rehabilitation, reconstruction, and development. In the first years after World War II this was in fact a unilateral effort in helping others, as far as the provision of the funds was concerned, even if the distribution of the funds was left to multinational co-operation. This was the pattern, by and large, of the United Nations Relief and Rehabilitation Agency (UNRRA), an international organization administering funds provided almost solely by the United States. In general, this was also the pattern of the Marshall Plan, supplying funds for the reconstruction of the economies of Europe, but leaving the allocation of the funds to the OEEC. Total expenditures through UNRRA between 1945 and 1947 were nearly $3 billion, of which $1.2 billion were for food, $400 million for textiles and footwear, $700 million for industrial rehabilitation, and $300 million for agricultural rehabilitation. Total Marshall Plan aid to Europe, in loans and grants, was almost $12 billion, of which $2.8 billion went to the United Kingdom, $2.4 billion to France, $1.3 billion each to Italy and Germany, $0.9 billion to the Netherlands, and $3.2 billion to eleven other countries. This generous program was instituted by the U.S. Congress through the European Cooperation Act of 1948. In the same year Congress passed two other, more modest, foreign-aid laws, the International Children's Emergency Fund Assistance Act and the China Aid Act.

Independent of these American-financed schemes of international economic co-operation, other programs were designed, instituted, and developed—programs which were international also with regard to the sources of funds. When, in the late 1950's, the financial over-exertion of the United States began to show up in an increasingly precarious balance-of-payments position, new types of financial arrangements had to be concocted, with the flow of funds less uni-directional. Some of the newer arrangements are so complicated, especially in their coexistence and interdependence with the older arrangements, that their description cannot be truly successful without another taxonomic exercise by which certain differences in their operation can be made more clearly recognizable.

Certain distinctions can be made regarding most of the arrangements under which funds are made available to a country:

Terms.—(1) grants, (2) equity investment, (3) long-term loans, (4) short-term loans.

Lending agency.—(1) international organization, (2) government agency, (3) monetary authority (central bank or treasury agency).

Receiving country.—(1) less-developed country, (2) industrial country, (3) reserve-currency country.

Direct recipient.—(1) government, (2) monetary authority (central bank or treasury agency), (3) investment bank, (4) deposit bank, (5) public enterprise, (6) mixed enterprise, (7) private enterprise.

Denomination.—(1) currency of receiving country, (2) currency of lending country, (3) currency of third country.

Occasion.—(1) development program, (2) investment project, (3) deficit in balance of payments, (4) temporary decline in export earnings, (5) speculative capital outflow.

Participation.—(1) multilateral, (2) bilateral.

Disposition over funds.—(1) funds immediately credited, disposable on demand, (2) funds made available upon request, (3) funds made available under certain conditions, (4) funds made available upon request conditionally after approval.

It would be much too cumbersome to classify all existing arrangements according to all these distinctions. We shall, however, find it possible to present a list of arrangements which embodies most of the distinctions and at the same time names the parties and organizations involved and describes the *modus operandi* of each scheme. (Descriptive statements from official publications of the organization are indicated by quotation marks.) The first two classes will include the best-known arrangements under which countries co-operate by making funds available: (A) long-term funds to less-developed countries and (B) short-term funds to countries in balance-of-payments deficit.

These will be followed by (C) co-operative interventions in foreign-exchange and gold markets and (D) consultation on use of funds and co-ordination of monetary policies.

A. Long-term funds to less-developed countries for the finance of development programs

1. International organizations

a) IBRD.—The International Bank for Reconstruction and Development, established in 1945, has now (September, 1963) 101 members and a capital subscription of $21,100 million. The Bank adds to its funds by issuing bonds. It "makes long-term loans in its member countries and territories to assist projects basic to economic growth—particularly in the fields of transportation and electric power—charging a rate of interest related to its own cost of borrowing a large proportion of its funds." From 1947 to the end of 1961, the Bank had made 316 loans in 60 countries or territories in an amount of $6,330 million, of which $4,560 million had been disbursed.

b) IFC.—The International Finance Corporation, established in 1956, has now 75 members and a capital subscription of $98 million. It "seeks to promote the contribution of the private sector to economic growth in its less developed member countries by investing—through loans, equity participation, or both—in significant private industrial enterprises on commercial terms." From 1957 to the end of 1961 the IFC had made 48 loans or equity investments in 18 countries in an amount of $64 million.

c) IDA.—The International Development Association, established in 1959 and starting operations in November 1960, has now 86 members and a capital subscription of $982 million. It "provides very long-term—e.g., fifty-year—development credits, with no interest payable, for a variety of development projects, including social projects, in those of its member countries whose need for development finance exceeds their capacity to borrow on conventional terms." By June 30, 1962, IDA had extended 22 development credits totaling $235 million in 11 countries.

d) UN Special Fund.—The Special Fund was established in 1959 by the Economic and Social Council of the United Nations to accelerate the economic and social progress of underdeveloped countries. In the three years 1959–61, 157 projects—38 in Africa, 46 in the Americas, 48 in Asia and the Far East, and 5 in the Middle East—were adopted at a total cost of $304 million, of which $131 million was to be earmarked by the Fund with finance pledged by the participating governments. The projects fall into three categories: (1) resources surveys and feasibility studies, (2) applied research projects, and (3) technical education and training projects. The executing agencies are the UN and "specialized agencies" such as FAO, UNESCO, ILO, etc.

e) EIB.—The European Investment Bank, established in 1958, has 6 members—the countries of the EEC—and a capital subscription of $1,000 million. The bank adds to its funds by issuing bonds. By the end of 1962, 22 loans had been granted in 5 member countries (54 per cent in Italy), in an amount of $160 million.

f) IDB.—The Inter-American Development Bank, established in 1959, has now 20 members and a capital subscription of $813 million. The Bank adds to its funds by selling bonds. Total loan commitments thus far are $618 million.

g) CABEI.—The Central American Bank for Economic Integration (BCIE, by its Spanish name), established in 1961 with a starting capital subscription of $12 million, provides funds for regional industrial development in the private sector and for public projects. In the first full year, 13 loans totaling $3.5 million were granted.

h) Alliance for Progress.—The Alliance for Progress, established in 1961 with 20 American member countries, is attempting a ten-year program of economic and social progress in Latin America. Immediate projects are for schools, school-feeding, health centers, water systems, housing, and farm-to-market roads; future projects include new industries, transportation networks, modernized agriculture. The outlays for the various programs in the fiscal year 1962 were $707 million. Finance has come chiefly from U.S. public funds, such as AID and EXIMbank.[29] Internal reform plans in the aided countries stress income-tax and land-tenure systems.

2. U.S. government agencies

a) EXIMbank.—The Export-Import Bank of Washington, an agency of the U.S. government established in 1934, has a capital of $1,000 million and may borrow an additional $6,000 million from the U.S. Treasury. It has the function of financing the foreign trade of the United States, chiefly through development loans "where credits for the purchase of United States equipment can be extended on a bankable basis." Total credits, guaranties, and insurance (through the Foreign Credit Insurance Association) during the fiscal year ending in June, 1962, amounted to $1,862 million.

b) AID.—The Agency for International Development is the agency of the U.S. government created "to assist other countries that seek to maintain their independence and to develop into self-supporting

---

[29] U.S. economic assistance to Latin America in the four fiscal years 1959–62 totaled $3,100 million.

nations." It was established in 1961 to take over the functions previously served by DLF and ICA (and, still earlier, MSA and ECA). It administers development assistance (loans, grants, technical co-operation, and the aid assistance for the Alliance for Progress and the Inter-American Program for Social Progress) as well as strategic assistance (military-assistance programs and "supporting assistance") and numerous contributions to the programs of other agencies. Total obligations and loan authorizations during the fiscal year ending June, 1962, amounted to $6,611 million (including $789 million from other U.S. agencies), bringing total economic and military aid to foreign countries since 1946 to $97,133 million.

B. Short-term funds to countries in temporary balance-of-payments deficit

1. Multilateral arrangements

a) *IMF.*—The International Monetary Fund, established in 1945, now has 102 members and a capital subscription of $15,540 million. It provides to its members drawing rights in amounts specified in quota regulations. Under these rights, deficit countries can buy foreign currencies with their own currencies, which they have to repurchase later with convertible currencies or gold. Between 1946 and April, 1962, the Fund put an equivalent of $6,266 million at the disposal of its members, of which $4,250 million had been repaid by April, 1962.

b) *Compensatory financing of export fluctuations of countries exporting primary products.*—The IMF, beginning in March, 1963, will provide drawing rights exceeding the ordinary quota regulations to member countries suffering temporary declines in their export earnings if "the Fund is satisfied that the shortfall is of a short-term character largely attributable to circumstances beyond the country's control and also that the member country will cooperate with the Fund in an effort to find, where required, appropriate solutions to its balance-of-payments difficulties." The first drawing under this arrangement was accorded to Brazil in June, 1963, in an amount of $60 million, in consideration of her reduced sales of coffee and cocoa in 1962.

c) *Compensatory financing of speculative capital outflows from industrial countries—"General Arrangement to Borrow."*—This arrangement, initiated in 1961 and concluded in 1962 at Paris, among 10 industrial countries—United States, United Kingdom, France, Germany, Italy, the Netherlands, Belgium, Luxembourg, Switzerland, and Japan—provides for a total of $6,000 million in stand-by loans by the monetary authorities of these countries to the IMF in order to augment IMF funds when required to meet the needs of any of the 10 countries whose currency is under heavy speculative attack. The loans, in the lender's own currency, will be granted upon request of the IMF, provided the lender country is satisfied that its own position is safe and the policies of the deficit country are sound.

2. Bilateral arrangements

a) Central-bank reserve accommodation for reserve-currency countries.—Certain central banks—such as the Deutsche Bundesbank and the Banca d'Italia—purchase and hold more dollars or sterling than they would carry for their own convenience, reducing thereby the customary ratio of gold in their foreign reserves. [This accommodation exposes the lending bank to an exchange-value risk.]

b) Central-bank special loans to reserve-currency countries.—Certain central banks—such as the Deutsche Bundesbank and the Swiss National Bank—lend their currencies to a reserve-currency country in deficit against its promissory notes repayable in currencies of the lending countries (DM, Swiss fr.). [This avoids the problem of an exchange-value guaranty to the lending bank.]

c) Credit swaps.—In bilateral arrangements two central banks lend their own currencies to each other, each lender crediting the borrower's current account, whose foreign-exchange reserve is thereby increased. Such arrangements have been made between the United States, on the one hand, and the United Kingdom, Canada, France, Germany, Italy, Belgium, the Netherlands, Switzerland, Austria, and Sweden, on the other.

d) Stand-by swaps.—In bilateral arrangements two central banks agree to extend to each other mutual credit facilities on a stand-by basis, that is, to lend each other their own currencies when requested in the future. Such arrangements have been made between the United States and some of the other countries mentioned above. The largest stand-by swap is the one between the Federal Reserve Bank of New York and the Bank of England in an amount of $500 million, arranged for in May, 1963. [The difference between "currency swaps" and "stand-by swaps" is analogous to the difference between money in the pocket and a charge account; though if the money in the pocket is only borrowed money, the difference between such cash and charge-account credit may not be great.]

C. Co-operative interventions in foreign-exchange and gold markets

1. Exchange rates

a) Forward-exchange transactions.—In bilateral arrangements two monetary authorities combine their interventions in spot and forward markets for foreign exchange, with a view to reducing the attractiveness of speculative capital movements. These interventions are often associated with unilateral or reciprocal loans, as was the case in 1962 in transactions of the Federal Reserve Bank of New York in concert with the Netherlands Bank, the Bank of Italy, and the Swiss National Bank. In order to avoid speculative dollar flows incited by a weakening of the forward rate of the American dollar, the New York Bank sells forward guilders, lire, or francs, after having secured the necessary cover through stand-by loans from the central banks concerned. The reduction of the spread between spot and forward rates also lowers the implied interest rates in the foreign markets and thus reduces the outflow of funds from the United States which is intended to take advantage of interest differentials.

2. Gold price

a) *Central-banks' Gold Pool.*—In an arrangement made in December, 1961, the monetary authorities of eight countries agreed to pool their resources to stabilize the price of gold in the London market. In order to control the London gold price within fairly narrow limits and thus discourage private speculation, the Bank of England, as manager of the pool, purchases all the gold offered by the Soviet Union and by private sellers, sells all the gold demanded by private buyers, and in monthly settlements resells to the members of the pool any surplus acquired or takes delivery from them to make up any deficit. The total commitment of the eight partners is $270 million, and their shares are as follows: U.S. $135 million; Germany $30 million; U.K., France, and Italy $25 million each; Belgium, the Netherlands, and Switzerland $10 million each. [In this fashion the burden of satisfying or discouraging private gold hoarders is equitably shared by the eight central banks.]

D. Consultation on use of funds and co-ordination of monetary policies
1. Advice on use of development funds.
2. Consultation on use of short-term loans.
3. Co-ordination of monetary policies.

International economic co-operation in the form of advice, consultation, and policy co-ordination might more appropriately come under the heading of "movement of ideas," a subject we cannot treat here, lest this essay grow to excessive length. But since the particular ideas concern the use of funds made available under the various arrangements enumerated above, it may not be improper to list the helpful precepts together with the helpful cash.

No explanations seem necessary concerning the copious advice embodied in reports, plans, memoranda, etc., to developing countries relating to their social, legal, military, economic, and technical projects. More should perhaps be said about the consultations between lenders and borrowers in connection with short-term loans to alleviate balance-of-payments pressures. For example, under the Fund agreement, a nation approaching the ceiling on its drawing rights is committed to listen to recommendations which the IMF may formulate for internal corrective policies such as budget reforms, fiscal restraint, and credit-tightening. Prescriptions of this sort may sometimes prove more important for the countries concerned than the short-term accommodations that tide them over until the remedial measures have the desired effects.

Discussions leading to co-ordination of the monetary policies of different countries are among the most significant developments in central banking. Co-operation among central banks is not a new invention; most writers on the subject give 1837 as the year in which such co-operation was practiced for the first time through a loan from the Bank of France to the Bank of England, and 1927 as the year in which co-operation was practiced through an accommodating change in domestic policy when the Federal Reserve Bank of New York adjusted its credit policy in order to ease the position of the Bank of England. The novel phenomenon is that the co-ordinating efforts are no longer limited to emergencies but are virtually continuous. The heads of the largest central banks meet every month at Basel, Switzerland, to discuss the situation—comparative liquidity positions, interest rates, payments imbalances, gold supply and demand, speculative capital movements, debt management, fiscal and monetary policies. Such "planned" co-ordination of central-bank policies was not needed in old times, when gold movements were accepted as the signals to be obeyed and the rules of the gold-standard game were generally adhered to. These times, remembered with nostalgia by many, are bygone. But if the central-bankers' club of today is composed of relatively conservative men, the results of agreed co-ordination are probably not very different from the "automatic" co-ordination that would be implied in actions dictated by the signals of the gold-flow mechanism. At any rate, since the orthodox gold standard is gone and since completely independent central-bank policies lead to trouble, the need for close contacts and continuous talks seems to be understood. To what extent genuine co-ordination of monetary policies could be achieved by discussion if the central bankers were of very different persuasions is still an open question.

CONCLUDING JUDGMENT

We should now be ready for a judgment, or at least an impression, concerning the importance and nature—quantity and quality—of international economic co-operation in the world today. Is there now *more* of it, relatively speaking, than there was in earlier times? Has it become more *genuinely* co-operative, less restrictive, less exclusive, less protectionist, less monopolistic, less discriminatory?

The first question can be answered with a confident "yes," no matter what quantitative indicators are employed. The number of (*a*) international conventions and agreements in force, (*b*) governments involved, (*c*) permanent organizations at work, (*d*) persons engaged in these activities, (*e*) persons affected by them, (*f*) commodities affected, and also the magnitude of (*g*) funds expended in these activities, and (*h*) trade affected by them have all surely increased not only absolutely but also relative to population, income, and trade volume.

It is the second question that gives us pause. Impressions may be very different according to the area of co-operation on which one focuses. In some areas one may be impressed with the generosity, unselfishness, and neighborly spirit of the co-operative activities; in others, however, one can see that co-operation is chiefly, as it always used to be, combination to restrict competition, a co-operative way of protecting some by excluding others.

The latter tendency is especially strong in the co-operative arrangements about trade in agricultural products but strong also regarding manufactured products. Good public relations by the international organizations in charge of regional trade systems have succeeded in creating an image of splendid "liberalization" for their schemes which in fact are rather protectionist and discriminatory. Complete abolition of tariffs among the countries within a region, coupled with a high external tariff, diverts some of the existing trade and creates some new trade. Generally speaking, trade diversion is harmful, and trade creation beneficial, on balance. The point to bear in mind is that a general tariff reduction of 20 or 30 per cent may create as much new trade as a 100 per cent reduction, that is, as the abolition, of intra-regional tariffs. If one considers that a regional system creates a new bureaucracy, new red tape, and new opportunities for cartelization, a comparative evaluation of common-market co-operation and general tariff reductions will be clearly in favor of the latter.[30] The record

[30] Cf. Gottfried Haberler, *The New Trade Policy, European Integration, and the Balance of Payments* (Greencastle, Ind.: DePauw University, 1963).

of co-operation on the international movement of goods is not one of which the world can be proud.

The record concerning the movement of persons is better, especially in Europe. Evidently, scarcity of certain types of labor has been the chief reason for the willingness of countries to receive foreign labor in large numbers. If the domestic labor force has moved away from badly paid or less pleasant occupations, an inflow of foreign workers to take the vacated jobs is welcomed or, at least, not resisted. If, for example, household help and hotel workers become exceedingly scarce, foreigners in these occupations are not regarded as competition for the native workers. If, however, the inflow of foreign labor were to become so heavy that large groups of natives felt competitive pressures, effective resistance would soon emerge. The argument that the flow of workers from countries of lower productivity to countries of higher productivity would increase the combined income of all nations concerned would then no longer be appreciated, and the beneficent and mutually advantageous co-operation would soon grind to a halt.

The record is best with regard to the movement of funds. The remarkable increase in co-operation among central banks is evidently attributable to a feeling on the part of the monetary managers everywhere that serious difficulties in a few key countries may lead to a collapse of the entire international monetary system, with detrimental consequences for all. The most impressive of all co-operative activities is foreign aid, particularly development grants and loans. One may be skeptical about the efficiency and effectiveness of the efforts; one may point to blunders, waste, and corruption on both sides, by those giving and those receiving funds; one may hold that much better results could have been obtained with much less money had other methods been used; one may insist that all development efforts will fail if the population explosion is not checked by effective birth control; one may argue that the chosen patterns of centralized development planning are incompatible with the development of adequate safeguards of political freedom. All this may be true, but the fact remains that never before has there been so much sacrifice for the benefit of others, so much well-meaning and thankless generosity on the part of the richer nations for the sake of the poorer ones. It is on this score that one may say that international economic co-operation has become more "co-operative" in spirit.

KENNETH E. BOULDING

The Dimensions of Economic Freedom

FREEDOM is a troublesome concept and all the more important for being troublesome. It is not something which can be measured easily on a linear scale so that we can say, without equivocation, that one person or one society is more or less free than another. It is a concept which frequently has more emotional than intellectual content. We all use it to mean what is fine, noble, and worthwhile about "our side." It is significant, for instance, that *"Freiheit"* was one of Hitler's slogans; that the Four Freedoms, which now, alas, seem almost to have passed from public memory, were the watchwords of the Atlantic Charter; that Engels' great phrase, "The leap from necessity into freedom," is a powerful weapon of Communist ideology; and that Portugal, Spain, Haiti, and even Mississippi belong to the "free world." Amid such a confusion of tongues it is almost, but not quite, pardonable to be cynical. Cynicism, however, is never good enough. A confusion of tongues is a challenge to an intellectual enterprise to clarify the sources of the confusion and evaluate its consequences.

The confusion arises because freedom is a concept with more than one dimension, and all its dimensions are important. A great deal of unnecessary political controversy and many false images of the world arise out of the failure to recognize the existence of these various dimensions. A person or society may be moving toward more freedom on one dimension and less freedom on another. Under these circumstances it is not surprising if we concentrate on the dimension which is favorable to us and neglect the dimension which is not. Hence we get into seemingly irreconcilable arguments about the meaning of these movements, with each party perceiving himself as becoming more free and the other party as becoming less. In this paper I shall distinguish three major dimensions of freedom which I shall symbolize by the names power, law, and understanding. These three dimensions almost certainly do not exhaust the concept; they

KENNETH E. BOULDING is Professor of Economics at the University of Michigan.

do, however, seem to represent the three *major* dimensions, and the failure to distinguish among them seems to be the principal source of controversy.

The first and most obvious dimension of freedom is power, that is, the generalized ability to do what we want. Power in turn has a number of dimensions, depending on the social system in which it is embedded. I have elsewhere distinguished three major organizers of society, corresponding to three major subsystems within the larger social system, which I have called exchange, threats, and love. To each of these there corresponds a dimension of power. In terms of the exchange system, power is purchasing power and is equivalent to wealth or riches. The richer a person or a society is, the more commodities can be commanded, the more can be bought of that which is offered for sale, and the more can be produced that has exchangeable value.

The second dimension of power relates to the threat system. Power here signifies the capability of doing harm and the capability of preventing another from doing harm to one's self. This is a complex and unstable system with some very peculiar properties, very little explored by social scientists. Violence is an important, though not the only, aspect of this system, and the institutions of national defense are of course its main organizational embodiment. Whereas in the exchange system we increase our power by increasing our ability to do things which others regard as good for them, that is, by being productive, in the threat system we increase our power by producing things which enable us to do to others what they regard as evil. For this very reason, exchange systems have a much better chance of being positive-sum games in which the total of everybody's welfare constantly increases, and threat systems tend to pass over into negative-sum games.

The third dimension of power relates it to what might be called the "integrative system." This is the kind of power which is given by status, respect, love, affection, and all those things which bind us to each other. The power of the teacher over his students, who acknowledge his superior knowledge and ability to teach; the charismatic power of a political or religious leader over his followers; the power of a beloved parent or a respected friend—these are examples of this dimension. Power in this sense is also an important organizer of society, the study of which has again been much neglected. Integrative systems, like exchange systems, are likely to develop into positive-sum games in which everybody is better off. In general we may venture the hypothesis that threat systems, as embodied, for instance, in slavery, oppression, and conquest, have a low horizon of development; exchange systems, a much higher one; and the integrative systems, the highest of all.

In all these three systems, freedom or power must be measured by the distance from the party concerned of the boundary which separates what is possible to him from what is impossible. This I have called the "possibility boundary." Each individual, organization, or society stands, as it were, at any moment of time at a point representing the existing state of the world. There are a large number of other conceivable points representing other states of the world, and we can divide the set of conceivable states into two subsets, the possible and the impossible. The impossibility of the impossible may be for a number of different reasons. There are states of the world, for instance, which are technologically impossible to reach at the present time. I can be in Detroit tomorrow, but I cannot be on the moon. The exchange system imposes limitations on me depending on what I can afford. It would be technologically possible for me to be sunning myself in Hawaii tomorrow, but I cannot afford either the time or the money for this agreeable excursion. There are limitations likewise which are imposed by the threat system. It is technologically possible for me to refuse to pay my income tax next month, but I am constrained from advancing toward this delightful state of the world in part, at least, because of the threat system which is involved in the law and its sanctions. I would very much like to go to China, and I would be willing to afford both the money and the time to do this, but the law prevents me. The integrative system likewise imposes a boundary depending on my status and on my position in the whole web of personal and organizational relationships. For some reason which is a little mysterious to me, I seem to have the power, once suitable preliminaries have been arranged, to get up and make a speech in a perfectly strange city, and a few people, at any rate, will come and listen to me. This is a power not possessed by everybody, and it depends clearly on the position of the individual in the integrative system.

As the main subject of this paper is economic freedom rather than freedom in general, we should perhaps give particular attention to that aspect of power which is most concerned with economics, that is, wealth, or its converse, poverty. In the absence of any good measurements of power or of freedom, any propositions regarding which are the *most* severe limitations on freedom are debatable, but it can at least be argued with some cogency that the most severe limitation on freedom for the mass of mankind is sheer poverty. In spite of two centuries of rapid economic development in some parts of the world, most human beings still do not have the freedom to travel much beyond the confines of their native village. They do not have the freedom to have full stomachs and healthy bodies; they do not have the freedom to provide their children with education; and the most severe limitations which are imposed on them are imposed by the sheer scarcity of commodities. For the very poor, the economic limitation is so severe and constricts them in so small a living space that other possible restrictions on freedom, such as those arising out of political dictatorship, are like distant mountain ranges beyond the close, high wall of poverty which shuts them in. It is only as economic power is increased from this extremely low level at which so much of the world still lives that other aspects of power become important. The relations here are complex. It may be, for instance, that a change in a political relationship and an increase in political freedom may be necessary before a process can be set in motion which will eventually lift the burden of poverty. The poor themselves, however, have very little say in whether this happens or not.

The second dimension of freedom concerns itself not so much with power, that is, with the distance of the boundary which divides the possible from the impossible, as with the nature or quality of the boundary itself. A slave and a free laborer may be equally poor and equally impotent, and the boundary of possibility may be drawn tightly around them by their sheer poverty. They may both be unable to enjoy full stomachs, physical ease, wide sources of information, and travel. In one case, however, the boundary is perceived as the will of another, that is, the master, whereas in the other case the boundary is an impersonal one, imposed by the market.

I have identified this aspect of freedom with "law" with some hesitation, because the concept of law itself is certainly wider than the notion of the kind of boundary which forms the limits of power. The problem of law also includes more than the problem of freedom. It includes, for instance, justice, which is an independent and equally important object of social organization. Thus in the sense in which I am using the word it is perfectly possible to have an unjust law, but it still remains a law. The extreme opposite of law in this sense, perhaps, is "whim," which is irrational and unpredictable behavior, especially toward another.

The difficulties of measurement and even of conceptual clarity in this dimension are great, and it is hard to tell whether a man or a society has more or less freedom in this regard. We are faced here with a multidimensional network of interlacing relationships, and in a brief essay we cannot do more than point to some of the major problems. There is, for instance, the dimension of certainty or uncertainty about the position of the boundary which limits our power. Sometimes we do things which we think we have the power to do, and we turn out to be disappointed. One of the difficulties here is implied in the very notion of a boundary: as long as we stay well within the boundary it is very hard to find out where it is. The effort to find out where a boundary lies involves probing operations which may be costly and which may even result in an actual constriction of the boundary. Our image of the nature and quality of the boundary therefore is almost inevitably derived from hearsay, that is, from written or verbal information rather than from actual experience. Most of us stop, if not within the boundary of the law, at least within the boundary where we think the law will catch up with us. We all, almost without exception, break traffic regulations up to the point where we think it may get us into trouble. Frequently, a few detections and penalties may be necessary before we learn where that boundary lies.

Another quality of the boundary of freedom which is of great importance is the quality of legitimacy. This is a very puzzling concept which nevertheless is obviously of great importance in establishing social organizations and the course of social dynamics. A boundary is legitimate when it is accepted as just and proper by a person who is limited by it. We can regard it, perhaps, as a threat-submission system in which the submission is not merely made out of fear of the consequences of not submitting but is made because the system as a whole is acceptable and is considered in the interests of the person submitting. A good example of a system of this kind is taxation. Most of us submit to be taxed, not merely because certain penalties will be imposed if we refuse, but also because we recognize that taxation in some degree is necessary for our own welfare. If taxation were completely voluntary, a lot of people would escape it. I do not mind, therefore, being forced to pay taxes myself as long as everybody else is forced to pay them likewise. Here freedom—and a specifically economic freedom in the sense of the freedom to enjoy a larger income— is limited by the tax system, presumably, however, in the interests of a larger freedom, that is, most of us feel that we might have less income, if there were no tax system at all, than the net income we enjoy under a tax system. At this point the problem of freedom seems to be inseparable from that of justice, for only limitations of individual freedom which are seen as just are likely to enhance this freedom in the long run.

Many of these problems fall into a category which might be called problems of conflict resolution. These are problems which arise when the power of one person or organization limits the power of another. Conflicts of this type all arise out of scarcity in some sense, where, if A succeeds in pushing his boundary of freedom away from him, this at the same time pushes B's boundary closer to B. A great deal of the political and organizational apparatus of society is concerned with situations of this kind. The institution of property, for instance, is a socially legitimated boundary system which divides a field of scarce goods into areas of freedom around each particular owner. Within limits, I can do what I like with my own. Property rights, of course, are never absolute and they are always created by society. The process of creating and limiting them, however, must also be legitimated, and this is one of the main functions of law. A good example of this kind of conflict resolution is a stop light at an intersection. The use of the intersection is scarce in the sense that two parties cannot occupy it at the same time. If there are no means of regulation, the exercise of the freedom of all is likely to result in the freedom of none —the parties will be dead. The traffic light creates property; it gives the right of way part of the time to travelers on one thoroughfare and part of the time to travelers on the other. It is inalienable property and not usually subject to exchange in the market, but it is property nevertheless, and when the fire truck comes by it may even be alienated. It is property, furthermore, which is established by some kind of legitimate process which is recognized as legitimate by all parties. Legitimate process is *due* process, which suggests, incidentally, why this concept is so important to civil liberties and to political freedom.

The constitution of a society is a set of rules for deciding conflicts. These rules may be either written or unwritten, and there are indeed always a good many unwritten rules which constitute, as it were, the tacit part of the social contract. Majority rule, for instance, is one such constitutional compact; in practice, however, it is always modified by unwritten restraints on the arbitrary power of the majority, for otherwise the social contract tends to break down. In the international sphere we still have no adequate social contract, and the development of a world social contract, whether written or tacit, is the highest-priority task of our time. Without this there is likely to be no freedom for anybody.

The "law" aspect of freedom, as applied to the particular arena of economic freedom, presents some problems of peculiar interest. In classical economic theory, the concept of perfect competition itself can claim to optimize the nature of the boundary which is imposed on individuals by economic constraints. In the first place, under perfect competition the boundary is not subject to the arbitrary whim of any person. Under perfect competition the seller faces many buyers; the buyer, many sellers; and if he cannot make a bargain with one he can make a bargain with another. Perfect competition is thus the state of affairs the furthest removed from slavery, in which the slave has no choice of master. The very existence of a labor market is an important guarantee of personal economic freedom and is a powerful check on the arbitrary power of organizations. In perfect competition, the economic power of the individual is limited by what seem to be impersonal forces, namely, the systems of relative prices which face him. It is true, of course, that these impersonal forces are the result of the aggregation of a large number of personal ones, but in the aggregation, at least, the arbitrary quality of personal forces is lost, and the individual is faced with a boundary which may perhaps be affected by the whims of fashion but is *not* affected by the whim of any one person. Under perfect competition, furthermore, economic conflict scarcely arises, simply because the range of bargaining is so small. Economic conflict arises between two parties over the terms of a bargain: where, for instance, a commodity is bought and sold for money, the seller would like to have a high price; the buyer, a low price. Under perfect competition, however, there is practically no occasion for conflict of this kind. If a seller tries to raise his price above the market, nobody will buy from him; if a buyer tries to lower his price below the market, nobody will sell to him. If, in addition, people are highly mobile between different occupations, there is practically no change in the state of the society which is capable of making one group of people permanently better off at the expense of another group. If a commodity suffers a loss of demand, or if it is taxed and becomes unprofitable to produce, those who produce it will simply quit their occupation and go and find another one, up to the point at which those who are left receive normal returns.

As we move away from perfect competition toward monopoly and—alas!—reality, the situation, of course, changes. Under monopoly, the quality of the boundary of freedom changes severely for the worse. The monopolist is felt to exercise a personal or organizational power over those who have to buy from him, for if there are no other sellers there is no way to escape the relationship. As we move toward bilateral monopoly, the situation gets even worse. Here economic conflict becomes intense and obvious; bargaining is difficult and costly and often breaks down; and each party has a sense of being limited by the will of the other, which is seldom regarded as legitimate. The problem of how to develop institutions by which the bargaining process can be legitimated in the case of monopoly power may be regarded as one of the major unsolved economic problems of our society. In the case of the unilateral increase in steel prices, for instance, there seemed to be no recourse but the presidential anger. In the case of a failure of collective bargaining in the labor market, as in the newspaper strike in New York City, there does not even seem to be this recourse. Once we get away from perfect competition, the whole process of legitimation of the relative-price structure is in total confusion. The arbitrary and confused nature, for instance, of the whole antitrust enterprise is a case in point.

The problem of legitimation becomes even more acute as we move from the exchange economy into what I have called the "grants" economy. A slowly increasing part of our economic life is governed by essentially unilateral transfers rather than by exchanges, which are bilateral transfers. In an exchange, something goes from A to B and something else from B to A. It is not always easy to tell a grant from an exchange; interest payments, for instance, have a good deal of the character of a grant in the short run but may be exchange in the long run. Tax payments have a good deal more of the character of a grant, although we can conceive ourselves as getting something rather tenuous for them. Subsidies, whether to industries or to individuals, and philanthropic donations clearly have the character of grants, though even here we have tricky cases. The support of the aged and also of the young can be regarded as part of a long-run exchange between those in middle life and those at the extremities. In youth and in old age we are recipients of grants, that is, we get more than we give; in middle life we tend to be makers of grants—we give more than we get. Part of this may be thought of as paying back what we received when we were young; part of it is paying out in the expectation of receiving grants when we are old. Even when we have eliminated all elements of long-run exchange, however, the grants system still looks pretty large. Here, unfortunately, we have practically no institutions of legitimation—indeed, practically no theory of what is legitimate, apart from some vague notions of merit. Philanthropy, whether public or private, seems to be a part of the economy where the rules are even less clear than they are in the case of antitrust legislation and prosecutions. The problem is hidden by the fact that the receipt of a grant always looks like an extension of the freedom of the recipient, whereas those who do not receive them are not conscious of any diminution of their freedom. In fact, however, insofar as resources are scarce, the giving of grants diverts resources from the non-receivers to the receivers and hence represents a real economic conflict of which (and perhaps this is fortunate) we are not fully aware.

The third great dimension of freedom is freedom from error, both intellectual and moral. A man may have a lot of power, and the boundary which limits his freedom may enclose a wide field. This boundary, furthermore, may be subject to the full blessings of law and legitimacy and free from dependence on the will of another or from uncertainty and arbitrariness. This man, however, can still be the slave of his passions and his stupidities. The more power he has and the wider the boundary of his freedom, the more quickly he may be able to damn himself. The mere quality of the boundary itself and all the majesty of law assembled will not save him. This is a dimension of freedom which is not, I think, encompassed in the other two, and yet which can be neglected at our great peril, for freedom misused will soon be destroyed.

Here again we face a problem of formidable size and complexity. We cannot discuss freedom from error without knowing something about the nature of truth. Pilate may not have been jesting, and he might not even have got the answer had he stayed, but his question, "What is truth?" has lost little of its difficulty. Nevertheless there is something both appealing and meaningful in the idea that "Ye shall know the truth, and the truth shall make you free." Freedom in this sense means the ability to fulfil an image of the future. If my image of the world contains my being at a certain place on a certain date in the future, and if when that date arrives, I find myself where I expected to be, this is a fairly convincing demonstration that the relevant part of my image of the world was true. A difficulty arises, of course, in that all images of the future have a degree of probability attached to them, and the mere fact that a particular expectation is fulfilled says nothing about the correctness of that probability. My being at a particular place at a particular time may, in fact, have been very improbable, but if I am there, in fact, there is no way of finding out how improbable it was. The test, therefore, of both truth and freedom in this sense is the amount of disappointment in the long run. If I am constantly disappointed, it is clear that there is something wrong with my image of the world; what I think is truth must in fact be error, and in consequence my actual forecasts are constantly falsified by this ignorance.

Freedom in the first sense of power is, of course, highly dependent upon knowledge of the truth. That knowledge is power is no mere copybook platitude, but perhaps the first law of social dynamics. The technology which so enormously increases our freedom in the physical sense is a direct and obvious result of increased knowledge of the nature of matter, energy, and space. One may hope also that in human relations and social systems an increase in knowledge will lead to a social, political, and economic technology which will preserve us from some of the disasters of the past.

In regard to economic freedom, the major problem here is the relation of the prevailing image of the economic system, especially among important decision-makers, to its actual development. It is perfectly possible, of course, to do the right thing for the wrong reasons, and in economics this is not treason at all but just sheer good luck. Our own agricultural policy, for instance, which was based on what seems to me to have been a wholly mistaken view of the nature of economic justice and of the effects of altering the price system, in fact has turned out to be a powerful stimulus to technological development, not only in agriculture, but in the whole economy. It is quite likely that if we had known better we would have done worse. Ignorance is bliss, however, only in the short run and in stochastic processes. In the long run, ignorance can hurt us and only knowledge can save us. What Engels meant, I think, by the "leap from necessity into freedom" was that when man achieves an understanding of the dynamics of his own society, he can then develop an image of the future for that society as a whole into which it has the power to progress. Man is no longer then the object of blind social or natural forces which he cannot control, and he can move forward into a future of his own making. This is a noble idea and should not be rejected out of hand. In our day, indeed, it is accepted by all—except, perhaps, by the most unreconstructed obscurantists. It is one thing, however, to say that we *can* know the truth and quite another thing to know it. The difficulty here is that it is the convincing image which is powerful, and the convincing is not always true. A good many people have come along, among them even Marx and Hitler, and have claimed that *their* service was perfect freedom. Man has never lacked for false prophets. Furthermore, in the absence of a process of cumulative social learning it is very hard to learn to tell the false prophets from the true. Merely because it is difficult, however, the problem cannot be pushed aside. In a great many of these matters we cannot simply suspend judgment; we must act upon *some* view of the universe. The hope here, as I have suggested, lies in a careful, cumulative process of long-run information collection, processing, and dissemination which can do for social learning what the scientific method has done for our knowledge of the physical universe. This goal may seem a long way off, but there are signs that we are moving toward it.

The economic aspect of this third dimension of freedom relates, of course, to the growth of economic knowledge itself. This is seen, for instance, in relation to two of the major economic problems of our day, economic development and economic fluctuations. That extraordinary process of economic development which began to accelerate with such force in the eighteenth century, in the full tide of which we find ourselves today, was certainly not initiated by any conscious plan or any clear knowledge of the dynamics of economic systems. Its origins lie deep in latent and unconscious processes which can, perhaps, be understood in retrospect but which certainly were not and could not be understood at the time. Who would have guessed, for instance, that the turnip and the potato would have engendered so great a revolution? The failure of economic development in many parts of the world, however, indicates that it is not a necessary process and that the West may simply have been lucky. We are now, therefore, desperately trying to understand the nature of this process in order that we may prescribe what needs to be done in those parts of the world that, to judge by results, have not yet done it. The full understanding of the process may not therefore be necessary to "lucky" economic development but may be necessary to make it certain and independent of luck.

Economic fluctuations represent an area where, in the Western world at least, an increase in economic knowledge has had a profound effect on the dynamics of the system. It would have been almost inconceivable, for instance, for Herbert Hoover to have proposed a substantial tax cut as a remedy for his depression. To do so requires not only a sophisticated economic theory—it requires an information-processing apparatus in the shape of econometric models and national income statistics which we simply did not possess thirty years ago. One of the critical problems at the moment, indeed, is that the image of the economy which is possessed by virtually all professional economists extends only a little way beyond their ranks; many of the people and perhaps even a majority of congressmen are operating with an image of the economic system which is so far removed from reality that we are in grave danger of being enslaved to our own ignorance and of failing to make our system operate successfully because those who have to make the important decisions do not possess the truth about it. On the other hand, we have to recognize that it is easy for economists to be wrong; that the truth about an economic system is very hard to obtain, especially in a system as complex as ours; and that there must be room for knowing when we don't know as well as when we do.

Beyond these matters of what might be called economic technology, there are more fundamental questions of the critique of values or objectives themselves, which not even the economists can escape, even though they frequently like to disclaim responsibility in this area. We do not have to go all the way toward believing in objective values and natural law to see that a critique of ends may be necessary even for quite positivistic social dynamics. Nazi Germany was fairly successful in solving the problem of depression and might even have done fairly well with economic development, but it used its freedom for such outrageous ends that it was destroyed. We cannot escape the fact, therefore, that there are ends which can destroy us, and it is important to identify them. If we use wealth for futile idleness, for meaningless luxury, for corrupt gratifications, and for the expression of hatred and prejudice, then the richer we are the sooner we will be damned. Besides the knowledge of means, therefore, there must be a very real knowledge of ends, and if we do not have true ends we will be enslaved by false ones. In this sense, too, the truth makes us free; but in this sense also it is hard to come by.

By way almost of an epilogue, it may be of interest to test the theory of the dimensions of freedom which I have outlined above in terms of the current ideological struggle between the Communists and the "free world," to see if we can throw any light on where the argument really lies and on what the conflict is about. This exercise is all the more important because both ideologies claim to be champions of human freedom, and the differences between them, important as they are, are at times surprisingly subtle. The image which the Communist has of himself is that of a liberator of mankind from age-old error and poverty, even if in that process man must be temporarily subordinated to a dictatorship. In the mind of the West, these promises are false and have been disproved by painful experience, and ideologically, therefore, the West envisages itself as the defender of political freedom, individual rights to privacy and non-conformity, and economic development which is mainly private and based on these virtues. The struggle is deeply felt and represents, in many cases, honest differences on both sides. Evangelical fervor, however, can easily turn into xenophobic fury when it is frustrated, and in a world of nuclear weapons this presents a constant and present danger. Where great and noble words like "freedom" and "democracy" are used in different senses by both sides, there is danger of misunderstanding and, worse, mounting mutual frustration which can end only in violence. It may be something more than a mere intellectual exercise, therefore, to apply the concept of freedom as I have analyzed it to this outstanding problem of our day.

I have equated the first dimension of freedom with power, and economic freedom in this sense is wealth. It is now becoming apparent that economic development from poverty to wealth is not a property either of socialism or of capitalism as such, but of a process of cumulative social learning of the kind which increases the productivity of labor. This cumulative process of social learning depends more than anything else on the proportion of resources which are devoted to it and on the efficiency of their use. It has become clear in recent years that it is not the mere accumulation of physical capital which brings about economic development, but a restructuring of the form of that capital in ways which represent greater and greater quantities of information. The learning process in society as a whole in all its institutions, not only those of formal education, is therefore crucial to the whole movement. In this regard the argument between socialism and capitalism is largely irrelevant. If we think of capitalist societies as guided mainly by the market and the price system, and socialist societies as guided mainly by the budget and the economic plan, we see that while both the market and the budget are, under certain circumstances, agents of the social learning process, neither of them by itself is sufficient. Market-oriented societies are old enough so that we have a number of examples of unsuccessful market development as well as of successful market development, and the difference here, one suspects, lies largely in the nature of the non-market institutions. Totalitarian socialism is so young that we have not yet had time to experience any clear examples of socialist failure, mainly because existing socialist countries have encouraged the educational process on which economic development rests. I suspect, however, that we shall find cases of unsuccessful socialist development, perhaps even in China, and we shall see that from this point of view the argument between socialism and capitalism is in large part irrelevant. The United States certainly would never have been a success if it had not been for the large non-market element in its social system. On the other hand it seems pretty clear that the prejudice against the market in socialist countries is a real handicap to them, and that those socialist countries which can most successfully overcome it, such as Poland and Yugoslavia, are the most likely to make rapid development.

Freedom in its second dimension is measured by the rule of law, the development of legitimacy, and the successful resolution of conflicts. In this sense democratic capitalism gets very good marks and totalitarian socialism very bad marks, though totalitarian market societies, too many of which are included in the so-called free world, fare pretty badly too. Political liberty and the absence of spiritual monopoly are very precious aspects of freedom, and ones in which the socialist countries do poorly. It is a bad sign when one of the principal exports of a society is refugees. This is a sign of gross domestic failure to provide personal liberty, the rule of law, and successful conflict resolution. The socialist societies of East Germany and Cuba are particularly to be indicted on these counts. It is the great virtue of a market-oriented society that it lends itself to the rule of law, that it operates more successfully under conditions of political liberty and impartial justice, and that discrimination and the denial of civil rights are a severe economic handicap—as the southern states have found to their cost. In market-oriented societies, furthermore, there is likely to be a wide diffusion of economic power. Up to now at any rate, we have discovered no administrative devices which can solve this problem in a socialist state, where all the economic activity in the society is concentrated in a single firm, which is the state; where the concentration of economic power in the matter of decision-making reaches its height; and where mistakes on the part of a few powerful individuals can cause universal suffering. In the absence of a true labor market, the almost inevitable limitations on the right of the individual to change jobs can easily be a more fundamental limitation on individual freedom than the deprivation of political liberty. When we add to this the denial of the right of the individual to start enterprises of his own, or to hire labor, or to create organizations outside the monopoly of the one-firm state, simply because of a theology of surplus value, we can see the socialist state as imposing limitations on individual freedom in which the boundary is of very low quality, often arbitrary and essentially meaningless.

On the other hand, we must not underestimate the ability of the socialist state to acquire legitimacy in the minds of its citizens. With the exception of East Germany and Czechoslovakia, there is no widespread alienation or denial of legitimacy in the socialist camp, even among those, like the Christians, who are discriminated against. It seems to take an enormous amount of discrimination to create alienation, as the experience of the Negro in the United States, the Christian in the socialist states, the outcastes of India, and the eta of Japan seems to indicate. Legitimation, however, is a variable that is very hard to evaluate. The Tsar of Russia seemed unshakably legitimate in 1914, in spite of widespread dissent. The Emperor's legitimacy in Japan survived an even more shattering defeat and occupation.

In the third dimension of freedom, in which freedom is equated with "truth" or a correct view of the world, there is obviously plenty of room for controversy. One can concede this much to Marxism: that the idea of social self-consciousness, that is, the idea that society as well as an individual can have a realistic image of its own future into which it can progress, is an idea of far-reaching importance for the whole future of mankind. In a sense, like a great many things in Marxism, it goes back to Adam Smith, whose *Wealth of Nations* is largely a study of the "progress of society" and how to get it. To say that a society *can* have such an image, however, is not necessarily to give it a true one. The Marxist image, in particular, is a case so special that for most societies it is grotesquely untrue. It involves an absurdly oversimplified notion of class structure, a fallacious view of the dynamics of the distribution of income, and a quite insufficient appreciation of the ability of capitalist society to develop itself along evolutionary lines while still retaining its essentially market-oriented character. The fact that Marx's own predictions have been largely falsified is well known. Communism has come, not in the countries of advanced capitalism, but in countries of very early capitalism which have a strong feudal and "folk" residue. Its success, insofar as it has been successful, has not been the result of appeal to class conflict, which has been almost universally disastrous, but in its ability to keep real wages low or even declining; to exploit the present generation ruthlessly, presumably for the benefit of the future; and its determination to devote large resources to education and investment in people. Communist development, however, has been achieved at a high social cost not only in terms of class war, refugees, the extermination of whole groups in society, and social disorganization but also in terms of the atrophy of much artistic and intellectual life, in the development of a harsh, barren, provincial puritanism, full of false values and heavy sentimentality, without even the grace notes of religion. The Communist's image of the world is quite reminiscent of that of the Prohibitionist, with its oversimplified and unduly moralistic approach to complex social problems. It is, of course, changing, and mostly for the better. One hopes for the rise of a liberal generation, as a result of so much investment in higher education, who will revolt against sterile austerities and moralistic platitudes. In the present generation, however, the oversimplified and distorted view of the social system which the decision-makers in these societies possess has involved them in severe social costs and grave errors.

By contrast, capitalist society frequently has no general public image of the future at all. The strength of a market economy lies often in the fact that there is, indeed, a "hidden hand," and that, as Adam Smith remarked, the market itself exhibits a tendency toward health which even the greatest absurdities of governmental doctoring cannot quite overthrow. On the other hand, capitalist society is also subject to certain diseases which the mere operation of the market mechanism itself cannot cure. It does not necessarily distribute income or even the fruits of progress in such a way as to prevent the alienation of large numbers of its people, as we saw in Cuba. Without any governmental stabilization, the market mechanism is subject to essentially meaningless fluctuations which can cause unnecessary loss and distress. It is not clear also that the market-oriented society will necessarily devote enough of its resources to social overhead and the investment in human capital to guarantee a sufficiently rapid rate of development. For all these reasons, knowledge of society itself is needed. Right-wing capitalists frequently have an image of society which is as grotesquely unrealistic as that of the Marxists and which can have equally disastrous consequences. There are, indeed, striking similarities between the right and the left. They are both impatient and moralistic, eager for short cuts, and unwilling to take the long, hard road that leads to truth. The conservative whose image of his own society is untrue, no matter how much he loves it, will not be able to conserve it, just as the revolutionary whose image is untrue will not be able to reform it. In both socialist and capitalist societies, therefore, deeper understanding is the key to freedom in the third sense. Freedom, if I may be pardoned for parodying Holy Writ, is power, law, and understanding; and the greatest of these is understanding.

In all these various dimensions then, is there any way in which it makes sense to say that there can be a "policy" about freedom? For some people the very idea of a policy for freedom may seem contradictory, for to them freedom means the absence of policy. It will be clear from the above that I do not hold this view and that though some freedom grows wild in the great jungle of social species, it flourishes best when it is intelligently tended. In each of the three dimensions which I have outlined above, therefore, I would argue that a policy for freedom is possible. It is possible to have an image of the future in the furtherance of which present decisions are made, and in that future, freedom in any or all of its senses may grow. Policy in this sense is not a monopoly of government, for decisions of private persons also may be taken in the light of an image of a future of increasing freedom. Government also, however, may be a servant of freedom as well as its enemy, and one of the great objects of political development is precisely to learn how political institutions may be devised and used in the service of freedom. But if political power and, still more, military power are often illusory and self-defeating, and if the law which is imposed from above often seems to destroy more freedom than it creates, the reasons must surely lie in our deficiencies of understanding. It is only as we come to understand the social system and the long-run dynamics of power that we can learn to use even coercion in the service of freedom, once that coercion is legitimatized and constrained. This once again points to the dimension of understanding as the greatest of the three, and the one without which the others will be in vain.

SEYMOUR E. HARRIS

U.S. Welfare Programs and Policies

How much of the output of the nation goes to welfare depends on numerous factors: e.g., the level and distribution of personal income, the productiveness of the tax system, the presumed need. At high and rising incomes, people tend to divert more resources to welfare, and serious declines may have similar results. In the great depression, with unemployment approaching 25 per cent and ten to thirteen million unemployed during some years and with the GNP down by one-third at the depression low, the pressure on government to provide resources for welfare greatly increased. Since 1940, such factors as the introduction of a much more progressive tax system; rising expectations in education which stimulated a widespread interest in adequate health services; the discovery of the effectiveness of insurance programs as a weapon for putting the costs increasingly on the beneficiaries; and the acquiescence of the American people to increased consumption taxes as a source of finance for welfare when the direct tax system reached a saturation point, with marginal rates for income taxes at 91 per cent and an 80 per cent over-all ceiling—these are probably the most important factors tending to stimulate outlays for welfare since 1940.

Much also depends on the competition for the tax dollar. Thus in 1961, with national defense and international relations absorbing almost $50 billion of the total expenditures of federal, state, and local governments of $165 billion; natural resources, absorbing $11 billion; highways, $10 billion; and interest on debt, $9 billion; the competition for education ($21 billion) and health and hospitals ($6 billion) was serious indeed. But public outlays for education and health improved more than all expenditures in the preceding four years (1957–61). Priorities for defense and space under Kennedy greatly limited the

SEYMOUR E. HARRIS is Littauer Professor of Political Economy at Harvard University.

expansion of outlays for other categories in the first three years of his administration.

Both the total amount and the expenditures by categories depend to a considerable extent on the value system of the American people and its representatives in the Congress. To some extent, the Congress will not reflect the views of the people; this seemed to be true of the Medicare program in 1962, if the polls are to be believed. Congressman Mills, Chairman of Ways and Means, probably is more influential on this issue than tens of millions of voters. But there clearly has been a preference, widely held in the early 1960's, to spend more publicly out of additional resources for defense and space than for welfare.

Under welfare expenditures I include both public and private contributions, with the major categories including health, education, and social insurance. The amounts involved have been growing at a very rapid rate, for example, $6.5 billion for the public programs in 1934–35 and $57.9 billion in 1960–61. These increases are related to the rising price level and standard of living. In fact, in spite of the tremendous increase in the public programs, they equaled only 14 per cent of GNP in 1960–61, compared with 12 per cent in 1934–35.

Total public and private expenditures on health, education, and other welfare were: in 1950, $35.165 billion; estimated for 1962, $95.230 billion, the respective percentages of GNP being 15 and 22. The larger increase suggested by the over-all public and private expenditures can be explained by the somewhat more rapid rise of private expenditures and also to some extent by the unusually large expenditures in the fifties for health, education, and social insurance. Beginning with the great depression and accelerated by the effects of World War II, welfare outlay has tended to increase at a marked rate.

Despite the fact that the federal government has the most productive sources of revenue, the federal proportion of total outlay for public welfare increased only from 45 to 47 per cent of the total from 1934–35 to 1960–61. Heavy military and related burdens falling on the federal government undoubtedly explain to some extent the small relative rise for the federal government.

FINANCING THROUGH INSURANCE

To the extent that welfare outlays involve insurance features, the large increases are not as burdensome as they seem to be. Social insurance, for example, increased from 6 per cent of the public total in 1934–35 to 39 per cent in 1960–61.

Indeed, there are problems raised by the social insurance programs, and in particular by the Old Age and Survivors Disability Insurance program (OASDI). It is a cardinal principle of this particular program that the benefits should be made available to the present old as well as to the present young when they become older. Therefore, during a transitional period of many years, the old tend to receive benefits much beyond what is justifiable on actuarial principles. It has been estimated by one expert that if taxes were to cease under the social security program at the present time that payments could cover only 25 per cent of the commitments. Some way will have to be found to return to the Old Age and Survivors and Disability Insurance fund the money that has been paid out to the recent-current old and the near-future old which they have not earned. This recoupment is not as troublesome as it might seem to be because the recovery of the amount of money involved will be less of a burden, say, twenty or thirty years from now when total incomes are much larger. But a reservation is required here, for as large sums of money are diverted in order to provide the recent and current old with adequate annuities, interest payments on the withdrawn sums are lost.

It is important to distinguish between the programs that are financed by the general taxpayer and those that are financed by the use of insurance and trust funds. When the taxpayer is asked to pay the bill, say, for the various programs of the veterans, this of course does involve a burden on the general taxpayer. But if, as is occurring today, roughly $12 billion are paid in payroll taxes to finance OASDI and an equal amount is then disbursed as benefits, the net effect is a transfer of resources or command of resources from those who pay the taxes to those receiving benefits.

In this connection consider a rise of federal budget expenditures from $37.7 billion in the 1950 calendar year to $84.5 billion in 1961, or a rise of $47 billion, compared with $42 billion of cash payments in 1950 and $104 billion in 1961, or a rise of $62 billion. The difference of $15 billion is explained largely by the disbursements of the various trust funds. These do not involve a burden on the economy in the same sense that other expenditures do, for they are not reflected in increased demands on the general taxpayer. To a considerable extent the beneficiaries finance their programs.

How much is made available for welfare depends partly on the ideology of the American people and partly upon the national income and its distribution. For example, in 1962 it is estimated that $25 billion will be spent for education, and some 82 per cent will be spent publicly and 18 per cent privately. Again, $31 billion will be spent for health purposes, 25 per cent by the public and 75 per cent under private auspices.

Welfare Patterns: U.K. and U.S.A.

Should we compare our pattern of spending for welfare purposes with that of the British, we would discover significant differences. For example, about 90 per cent of the British expenditures for medical purposes passes through governmental channels and only 10 per cent through private sources. Moreover, the British spend considerably less relatively for veterans' benefits than is spent in the United States. The difference here undoubtedly is related to some extent to variations in governmental systems. In the United States the influence of groups seeking special treatment is likely to be much greater than in Britain with its parliamentary system—hence, the more favored treatment of veterans here. Again the American people put a higher value on making education available to the masses than do the British and hence have tended to spend relatively more for public education.

Welfare Programs and Tax Systems in the United States

To some extent the expenditures under various categories depend upon the leadership shown by the federal government. For example, the federal government has spent large sums of money for highways and public assistance and also large amounts for health, but on the whole has neglected education. Through grants-in-aid the federal government can greatly influence total amounts spent for different categories. State and local governments tend to spend more in areas where they can get a substantial amount of help from the federal government.

How much is spent and by what levels of government depend on the tax system. For example, in 1961, of the $77 billion of tax money raised by the federal government, corporate and income taxes accounted for $62 billion. These respond well to rising income. It might, therefore, be expected that the federal government would spend a rising percentage on welfare programs. This is especially to be expected in view of the fact that of $39 billion collected by the state and local governments, the general property tax accounted for $18 billion; and direct taxes, such as corporate and income taxes, $4 billion; and largely consumption and sales taxes for the remainder. Sales taxes, in particular, and the general property tax do not respond to rising income nearly as well as do income and corporate taxes.

Yet state and local governments have tended to increase their expenditures in recent years more than the federal government. Thus, from 1952 to 1962, the estimated rise of total expenditures of the federal government was from $72 to $110 billion, an increase of roughly 50 per cent, and for state and local governments from $25 to $59 billion, an increase of roughly 135 per cent.

One looking forward, say, in the 1940's would scarcely have expected this surprising development of a much larger increase of state and local government expenditures than of federal. Part of the explanation lies in the fact that the general property tax, which yielded approximately $20 billion in 1962, or close to one-half of state and local tax revenues, has been much more flexible and elastic than had been anticipated. This is explained partly by the large amount of building since World War II and also by the more realistic assessments of property values in many cities.

TABLE 1

STATE AND LOCAL PER CAPITA GENERAL EXPENDITURES, TOTAL AND SELECTED
FUNCTIONS, AND PER CAPITA PERSONAL INCOME, 1959*

(Ranking)

State	All General Expenditures	Local Schools	Higher Education	Highways	Health and Hospitalization	Public Welfare	Police and Fire	Per Capita Income
California....	3	3	1	30	6	5	5	6
Massachusetts	21	38	49	32	3	7	2	10
Mississippi...	42	43	21	29	43	18	49	50
Texas........	36	29	26	25	45	33	26	31

* Bureau of Census, Governments Division, mimeographed, n.d.

Looking ahead, one might well expect that the contribution of state and local governments will continue to rise in the 1960's, perhaps more that that of the federal government, at least in the welfare area. It should be noted, however, that the increase in indebtedness of state and local governments in the last ten or twelve years has been quite serious and has been rising at a much greater rate than that of the federal government. The rise of indebtedness may restrain state and local outlays in the next ten or fifteen years.[1]

WELFARE OUTLAYS AND VALUE SYSTEMS

Allocation of welfare expenditures, state by state, depends to a considerable extent on the value systems of the people and their governments. In this paper I present a table which compares the ranking of four states—Massachusetts, California, Mississippi, and Texas—on the basis of all expenditures and several welfare categories, as well as per capita income. For example, California is ranked third for general

[1] The fiscal material used so far comes from United States Census, *U.S. Governmental Finances in 1961* and the *Economic Report of the President* (January, 1962).

expenditures per capita, sixth for per capita income, third for expenditures on local schools, first for higher education, and sixth for health and hospitalization expenditures. In other words, California stands up well in relation to its per capita income in all categories of spending except highways, where she is ranked thirtieth.

Texas' rankings are fairly consistent with those for her per capita income, where her rank is thirty-first. In all general expenditures she is somewhat low at thirty-sixth, in schools and higher education, twenty-ninth and twenty-sixth, and in other categories not too far away from her rank in per capita income. But she is only forty-fifth in health and hospitalization.

Massachusetts is way behind in schools and higher education, being ranked thirty-eighth and forty-ninth against per capita income of tenth, but she ranks very high in health and hospitalization, public welfare, police and fire, third, seventh, and second, respectively.

In California, for example, there is a strong tradition of education, as is reflected in her large expenditures on education. In Massachusetts it is held that the large Catholic population, which has very heavy recourse to private schools, tends to discourage public expenditures on education. This may be part of the explanation of the low expenditures on education in Massachusetts. In contrast, the state is way ahead of what might be expected in her outlays for health and hospitalization and public welfare, particularly assistance payments. In police and fire she is almost at the very top, and this is held to be the result of excessive padding of payrolls, with Boston, for example, using more policemen and firemen in relation to its population than any other city, smaller or larger.

MAKING THE BENEFICIARIES PAY

How much will be spent on welfare depends to some extent upon the tax systems used. Much has been said about the large welfare expenditures in Great Britain, particularly in view of the low per capita income which, on the basis of relative purchasing power (exchange rates adjusted to measure relative purchasing power of the dollar and sterling), may be put at about 50 per cent of the United States' per capita income. But the British are able to introduce such ambitious welfare programs because they put a much larger part of the tax burden on consumption than governments do here. For example, the National City Bank, in its *Monthly Letter* (October, 1962), pointed out that taxes on consumption at all levels of government in fiscal year 1960 were 22.3 per cent for the United States and 35.7 per cent for the United Kingdom. (The latter figure is for fiscal year 1959.) In a sense, what the British have done is to put a heavy burden of taxation on consumption, thus discouraging the consumption of alcohol, tobacco, luxuries and using the proceeds to provide services, such as health, housing, and education. One investigator put the issue as follows:

The outstanding feature of the postwar growth in redistribution is not that of taking from the "classes" and giving to the "masses." The main feature is that the benefits of redistribution cut across income groups and are largely related to consumption. As a general proposition the working class pays enough additional in beer, tobacco and purchase taxes, and other indirect levies to meet the increased cost of the food subsidies and health and education expenditures, while the increase in direct taxes they pay covers the rise in their transfer money receipts. Those who do not smoke or drink, but live in a government owned house, wear utility clothing, use utility furniture, and have a large family, enjoy the maximum of benefits and pay the minimum of taxes.[2]

DISTRIBUTION OF INCOME AND CONSUMPTION

It might have been expected that in view of the rising standard of living and the improved distribution of income in recent years that the proportion of income going to welfare services would have been reduced, but this has not happened.

Both in the United States and in the United Kingdom, this improvement of distribution is to be seen. Thus, the percentage increase in the U.S. from 1941 to 1950 for the average family personal income after individual income-tax liabilities (by quintiles, going from those with the lowest incomes to the highest quintiles and to the top five per cent) was as follows: 42, 37, 24, 16, 8, and minus 2, and for all incomes combined, a rise of 17 per cent.

One investigator found that from the years 1938 to 1948 the working classes in Great Britain increased their consumption of goods and services by 22 per cent; the middle class experienced a reduction of 18 per cent; and the wealthy class, a reduction of 42 per cent, or a total increase of 6 per cent.[3] The explanation of these changes in distribution of income and consumption lies partly in the changing tax structure and partly in reduced unemployment.

---

[2] F. Weaver, "Taxes and Redistribution in the United Kingdom," *Review of Economics and Statistics*, XXXII (August, 1950), 201–3. A. T. Peacock, *The Economics of National Insurance* (London: Wm. Hodge & Co., 1952), pp. 67–72. *National Policies for Education, Health and Social Services* ("Columbia University Bicentennial Conference Series" [Garden City, N.Y.: Doubleday & Co., 1955]), pp. 363–66.

[3] Weaver, *op. cit.*, p. 212. Selma F. Goldsmith *et al.*, "Size Distribution of Income since the Mid-Thirties," *Review of Economics and Statistics*, XXXVI (February, 1954), 26.

WHY RISING OUTLAYS

That nevertheless there has been a significant increase in the proportion of expenditures for welfare is explained by numerous factors. One is, of course, the impact of a more progressive direct tax program which makes it possible for government to spend larger sums of money. The second factor is that with rising income there is a greater desire for improved education, health, and housing. Third, the rising per capita income in itself makes it easier for the government to make larger levies for welfare. Finally, under the pressure of this demand for welfare services, the government can justify increases in taxes on consumption, as is evident in the British tax system and also in the tax systems of our state and local governments.

WELFARE POLICIES AND THE STATE OF THE ECONOMY

Spending for welfare has also been related in the last generation to the problem of keeping the economy healthy. A theory largely developed by J. M. Keynes held that in the modern economy there is often a shortage of demand, with the result that goods and services being produced cannot be sold at favorable prices. The therapy is largely in stimulating demand through public spending and investment.

Keynes has written:

Ancient Egypt was doubly fortunate, and doubtless owed to this its fabled wealth, in that it possessed *two* activities, namely, pyramid-building as well as the search for the precious metals, the fruits of which, since they could not serve the needs of man by being consumed, did not stale with abundance. The Middle Ages built cathedrals and sang dirges. Two pyramids, two masses for the dead, are twice as good as one; but not so two railways from London to York. Thus we are so sensible, have schooled ourselves to so close a semblance of prudent financiers, taking careful thought before we add to the "financial" burdens of posterity by building them houses to live in, that we have no such easy escape from the sufferings of unemployment. We have to accept them as an inevitable result of applying to the conduct of the State the maxims which are best calculated to "enrich" an individual by enabling him to pile up claims to enjoyment which he does not intend to exercise at any definite time.[4]

For example, why not pull down the whole of South London from Westminster to Greenwich, and make a good job of it—housing on that convenient area near to their work a much greater population than at present, in far better buildings with all the conveniences of modern life, yet at the same time providing hundreds of acres of squares and avenues, parks and

[4] J. M. Keynes, *The General Theory of Employment, Interest, and Money* (New York: Harcourt, Brace & Co., 1936), p. 131.

public spaces, having, when it was finished, something magnificent to the eye, yet useful and convenient to human life as a monument to our age. Would that employ men? Why, of course it would! Is it better that the men should stand idle and miserable, drawing the dole? Of course it is not.[5]

But in the last twenty years or so, recourse to increased public spending as a means of stabilizing the economy and increasing the rate of growth has become less fashionable. For example, in the 1964 Budget of President Kennedy, the stress is not on increasing non-military spending but on reducing taxes as a means of stimulating the economy. In fact the rise in the 1964 Budget can be explained by the increased expenditures for military and space programs. When one considers that annual average increase in wages is about 3 per cent; in population, 2 per cent; and in prices, 1.5 per cent; it might be expected on the average that the total budget would rise by about 4 per cent in the year without any new programs or extensions of old programs. Therefore, when the President announces that he has increased the budget by roughly the amount of spending on space and defense, he has in fact reduced his real expenditures on welfare and other non-military purposes.

One may ask why the shift to tax reduction for stimulating the economy instead of an increase in expenditures for welfare and similar purposes. One reason is that the reduction in taxes has a much greater political appeal. A second point is that in the 1930's, when the public-spending approach was used in this country, it was not very helpful, in part because of delays in identifying appropriate programs and in getting them through and partly because of the difficulties of synchronizing outlays with economic conditions. In recent years economists have become more dubious of the spending program because in actual practice the kind of spending programs that are easy to put across, such as programs for veterans and agricultural support prices, do not appeal to the economist. Those who, like Galbraith, want extension of public programs seek public investments in education, housing, health, transportation, and development of our natural resources. But these are the areas where rises of expenditures are more difficult to achieve.

What is significant here is that the popularity of tax reduction, as opposed to more spending as a method for treating stagnation, cyclical indispositions, or acceleration of growth, means reduced welfare programs. Galbraith, for example, is against tax reduction because to him it means less spending on welfare programs. His value system stresses the need of more public spending relative to private spending.

One objective of the appropriate program, whether it be increased

[5] J. M. Keynes, *Essays in Persuasion* (New York: Harcourt, Brace & Co., 1932), pp. 153–54.

spending or tax cuts, is to reduce the excess amount of unemployment. In this respect it may very well be desirable, insofar as possible, to concentrate on the direct approach, that is, for example, bringing jobs to the depressed areas or retraining workers who are out of jobs. Under the Manpower Training Act, for example, the government trains a man at the cost of about $1,000 per man and only goes ahead if there is a job in prospect for the man. Should one compare these costs with the costs of providing additional jobs under the fiscal policy approach, one would find that the fiscal policy approach is much more costly. Here, for example, are some assumptions and calculations:

1. From 1958 to 1961 there was an increase in the gross national product of $67 billion.

2. During the same period the number of jobs increased by three million.

3. Therefore, it may be assumed for this period that an additional million jobs involved an increase of gross national product of $22 billion.

4. It may be assumed that in order to achieve an increase of GNP of $22 billion through governmental fiscal poicy, an additional deficit of $11 billion would be involved. This suggests that for every dollar of deficit there would be a rise of GNP of two dollars. This is a multiplier that is very generally used, though there is a substantial element of error and uncertainty here. At the rate of $11 billion for a million jobs, the cost per job is $11 thousand, which is considerably in excess of the cost using the direct approach.

Where there is a large amount of unemployment, say in excess of 6 per cent, it becomes increasingly difficult to obtain jobs through retraining and similar programs. The retraining and other programs are effective only when there are unfilled vacancies. The higher the amount of unemployment, the fewer unfilled vacancies will be found. Hence, as potent as the direct approach is, there are limitations to its use.

PAYROLL TAXES AND THE ECONOMY

Estimated public expenditures for social insurance for 1962 are $23.6 billion. This is a large sum of money. The major programs (estimated) are OASDI, $14 billion; railroad and public employees retirement, $4.4 billion; Unemployment Compensation, (inclusive of employment service), $3.7 billion; Temporary Disability Insurance and Workmen's Compensation, $1.5 billion.[6] It would be helpful if these

[6] Figures from *Handbook on Programs of the United States Department of Health, Education, and Welfare* (Washington, 1962), Table 1.

large payments could be adjusted to the economic situation; that is to say, it would be preferable if a large proportion of the taxes were imposed in a period of prosperity and a large proportion of the benefits provided in a period of depression or recession. For example, the payroll tax might be adjusted according to the economic situation with variations, say, every three months. Unfortunately there is such great concern about the financing aspects, and especially the fear of exploiting or using up reserves, that the general position of economists and government is that there should not be any large variation in rates paid in response to varying economic conditions.

In the 1930's, the years of depression, there were large accumulations in the OASDI. This is just exactly what was not wanted, because it meant taking cash away from people who otherwise might have spent it. The result was, of course, that there were significant postponements of scheduled rises in the payroll taxes in order that the program might not further depress the economy. In similar manner, in 1963 there is scheduled a $2 billion additional tax burden through the increase in taxes under OASDI. Much could be said for postponing this increase. But here again the great concern over providing adequate revenue to meet the cost of the program without imposing taxes on the general taxpayer makes Congress reluctant to postpone this particular increase in the payroll tax.

There are, however, tendencies for some benefit payments to be increased when economic conditions deteriorate. For example, in the last two recessions approximately $2 billion more was paid out in each recession than in non-recession years. Moreover, we have on two occasions at least provided additional temporary unemployment compensation to treat substantial amounts of unemployment, and there have been efforts made to make this a permanent feature of the Unemployment Compensation program.

In view of the relationship of these programs to the economic situation there is indeed one unfortunate aspect of the Unemployment Compensation program. The rates are to some extent related to the experience of the employer with unemployment, a system generally referred to as experience or merit rating. The theory is that when unemployment is low, the employer is responsible and should be rewarded. Actually, of course, variations in unemployment primarily depend on general economic conditions. The individual employer can stabilize the employment of his firm relatively little. Unfortunately, this system results in much larger taxes in periods of high unemployment and smaller taxes in periods of low unemployment, exactly the reverse of appropriate policy. When unemployment is high, taxes should be low, with stimulating effects on the economy; and when unemployment is low, taxes should be high, with repressive effects.

One result of merit rating is that payroll taxes tend to be low and, hence, benefits low. This results in some states gaining a considerable competitive advantage over other states, and this is particularly undesirable in view of the fact that the objective of the federal program was to put each state in an equal, competitive position. The effective rate in 1962 was less than 1.5 per cent of total wages in covered employment. The net average concealed variations in individual employer rates ranged from zero for some employers in some states to 4.5 per cent for some employers in other states. On a state basis, average state taxes ranged from 0.64 per cent in Iowa to 3.23 per cent in Pennsylvania.[7]

PRIMARY AND SECONDARY EDUCATION

Of the estimated expenditures, public and private, for health, education, and welfare of $95 billion in 1962, $31 billion were for health and $25 billion for education. Almost 60 per cent of the total expenditure for welfare is allocated between these two items. I shall, therefore, concentrate on education and health in the remainder of this paper and discuss some of the relevant issues of policy.

As we shall see, the cost of education, related to the rise of prices and of productivity in the economy, has grown at a very rapid rate. In primary, secondary, and higher education one of the problems is that the schools and colleges have to face competition for men and services from other segments of the economy, and yet education does not achieve the gains of productivity that prevail in the economy generally. Hence higher prices and wages, not offset as much by rising productivity in education as in industry generally, means more inflation for the educational segment. Education is largely a personal process, and hence economies of scale are not as available in education as they are in manufacturing, agriculture, and many of the services.

Another general aspect of primary and secondary education is the fact that it is financed primarily by the general property tax. I refer to public school education, where the property tax finances 94 per cent of the total cost. The general property tax is not a highly elastic tax; that is, it does not respond too well to rising prices and incomes. Association of education with the general property tax tends to aggravate the financing problems of education. A related problem is the fact that primary and secondary education has become largely the function of the local government. These local governments depend

[7] Robert C. Goodwin, Director of the Employment Security Program for the U.S. Department of Labor, *Statement for the United States Treasury Group* (November 28, 1962).

primarily on the general property tax for their finances. In a recent year, public schools depended for their revenue to the extent of 56 per cent on local government, 39 per cent on state governments, and 4 per cent on the federal government. The unwillingness of the federal government to finance a substantial part of the bill has of course made the problem a more serious one.

It is often said that the schools are not very efficient. For example, schoolteachers are required to perform numerous menial tasks that might very easily be performed by assistants, thus saving large resources. Again, since about 80 per cent of the total expenditures on education are public, it might be inferred by many that the schools are usually inefficient because they depend on taxpayers' money and there is not the usual stimulus of balancing the budget when resources must be obtained from sources other than taxes. Again a reduction in the number of pupils per teacher—from thirty-seven in 1900 to twenty-seven in 1956—might also suggest reduced productivity to many. Unfortunately, it is not easy to estimate either the input or the output of the school system, and hence movements in the relation of the two, that is, trends in productivity, are difficult to judge. It is possible, for example, that an increase in the proportion of administrators in the school system and a reduction in the number of pupils per teacher may very well result in an improvement in the product. Again, the rising educational achievement of teachers undoubtedly contributes to an improved product, but it is difficult to measure the improvement in product.

The rise in the cost of public schools has been great. In 1900 total expenditures of public schools were $215 million, and by 1956, almost $11 billion. In these fifty-six years there occurred a doubling of enrollment and large increases in the number of days in the school year and in average daily attendance. An average increase in instructional salaries of twelve times meant that with prices rising for the nation by about three times, the gain of salaries in real purchasing power was more than 200 per cent.[8]

Increases in capital costs and in the proportion of high-school students are also relevant factors. For example, in 1910 the high-school enrollment was 5 per cent of the total public school enrollment, and by 1955–56, 22 per cent. Secondary schools are much more expensive than elementary schools per student. The average instructional cost per pupil at the salaries of 1958–59 was $103 in elementary schools and $243 in secondary schools. The ratio of teachers to pupils was

[8] S. E. Harris, *More Resources for Education* (New York: Harper & Bros., 1960), p. 14.

1:30 in elementary and 1:21 in secondary schools. The difference in teachers' salaries was $535.

In a recent period of several years, there was an increase in the public school bill of about 22 per cent in constant prices, and this roughly matched the rise in productivity of the economy. In other words, the schools have been keeping up recently with the economy in the allocation of resources.

It is of some interest that the National Education Association (NEA) estimated total expenditures of public schools at $12.3 billion in 1959–60 and projected that for a good school system with the number of pupils anticipated for 1970, which would provide the minimum quality of education, the cost would be $33.6 billion. In order to assure the quality target, the National Education Association assumed that the cost would rise from $321 per student to $720. In the absence of inflation, such increases are not likely to be forthcoming.

One of the problems confronting the schools is the relatively larger rise of enrollment as compared to that in population generally. In order to have high-quality schools, there is need for higher salaries and for additional classroom space. The schoolteacher, in fact, has re-established his or her economic position vis-à-vis the rest of the population compared to prewar. Salaries are generally sufficiently higher in relation to the prewar figure to match not only the increase in prices but also that in real per capita income (dollars of stable purchasing power). But with the shortage of teachers, increased demand, which emanates from rising enrollment and the desire to increase the number of teachers in relation to the number of pupils, may require a further substantial increase in teachers' salaries.

In 1959–60, the average pay of public schoolteachers was $5,135. This compared with the following salaries of those with similar amounts of education: chief accountants, $11,597; other accountants, $7,620; auditors, $7,701; attorneys, $12,144; chemists, $9,301; engineers, $9,797; all groups (eight in all), $9,474. The NEA suggests that a beginning salary of $6,000 and an average salary of over $10,000 would be required to do an adequate job in 1962. In the view of the NEA, the average teacher's salary in the early 1970's should be about $15,000.[9]

It will certainly be very difficult to obtain as much as $33 billion for public schools. A minimum figure for 1970, assuming a much larger school population and an increase in real resources per pupil

    [9] See especially National Education Association of the United States, *Financing Public Schools, 1960–1970* (Washington, 1962), especially chaps. 4 and 6 and pp. 133–35; National City's Citizens' Commission for Public Schools, *Financing Public Education in the Decade Ahead* (December, 1954); Committee for Economic Development, *Paying for Better Schools* (New York: 1960); Harris, *op. cit.*, especially pp. 12–20.

matching the rising productivity of the economy, would be $25 billion, or a rise of about $11 billion above recent levels. In addition, government may have to finance a $5 or a $7 billion increase in expenditures for higher education. This would mean an increase for education of about $16 billion. When this figure is compared with the increase in total outlays of state and local governments of from $21 to $50 billion over a recent ten-year period, or roughly from $21 to $40 billion in stable prices, one can see that it will not be easy to obtain. At present prices, education would have to absorb about four-fifths of the estimated increase in revenue of state and local government, and this assumes that the state and local governments can continue to increase their expenditures by $20 billion in stable prices, as in the last ten years. The amounts involved suggest that education should receive a proportion of the additional total expenditures considerably higher than its current proportion of total expenditures. In 1962 the estimated expenditures for education were roughly one-third of the total expenditures for welfare. The state and local government public expenditures for education were roughly 30 per cent of the total state and local expenditures in 1961.[10]

I have not said very much about the problem of private elementary and secondary education. I should point out, for example, that the parochial schools take care of five million pupils, and their average outlay is probably less than half of the average outlay of the public schools. This means a financial burden of about $2 billion and makes it much more difficult for the Catholic institutions to do a good job in higher education. These are the roughest of figures, I might add.

Higher Education

In higher education, serious economic and financial problems are with us. It is anticipated that enrollment in higher education will rise to about seven million within ten years, or three million in excess of current enrollment, and ten years beyond that, the problem will be even more serious. This rise of enrollment stems in part from the increase in the numbers of young men and women of college age and also from a steady rise in the proportion of those of college age who intend to go to college. Increasingly, as employers demand college education as a condition for entry, the demand for higher education increases. Often these demands for a college education are not justified by the job requirements; nevertheless, these demands are made.

In order to raise salaries of college teachers to a level which would

[10] Figures from *Handbook on Programs of the United States Department of Health, Education, and Welfare, U.S. Governmental Finances in 1961*, Table 1, and *U.S. Governmental Finances in 1962*, Table 2.

assure the number of teachers of requisite quality to take care of the additional students and keep pace with the general rise in the standard of living, colleges of this country will require $12 billion in the early 1970's for current operating educational expenditures as compared to $4.7 billion in 1959–60. This seems like a large increase but actually if the rate of growth from 1957–58 to 1959–60 or even for the preceding five or six years to the present continues, the resources will be available. In these two years the increase in educational income of institutions of higher learning was 25 per cent. Possibly the additional amount of money required may be somewhat less, especially if we rule out inflation entirely and also allow for the fact that the largest increases in enrollment are occurring in the colleges that are relatively low-cost colleges, for example, the junior colleges, the urban universities, and the large Catholic institutions. The relative enrollment in the Ivy League, other outstanding universities, outstanding liberal arts colleges, and women's colleges is steadily declining.[11]

In order to obtain these resources we shall have to depend on all significant sources, including tuition, government, gifts, and endowment income. In the late 1950's, tuition yielded about 25 per cent of income; government, 48 per cent; endowment income and gifts, 15 per cent; and other, 11 per cent. By 1970 the proportion of tuition is likely to increase and government's share to decline to some extent, though there should be an increase of more than 100 per cent in the total contribution of government. Endowment income and gifts should decline to about 12 per cent, with other income remaining about the same. These are not normative figures but rather rough estimates of what may happen.

It is possible that I have underestimated the potential contribution of state and local governments. Actually the rise of the contribution of government has been larger than I anticipated a few years ago. Much will depend, of course, on the particular conditions in different states. It is quite clear that the proportion of enrollment in public institutions is likely to rise. In the 1950's public enrollment increased from about 50 to 60 per cent. In 1970 or 1975 we should have 70 to 75 per cent of all college students in public institutions. Under pressure from students and alumni, the state governments are likely to increase their contribution. Much depends on the tradition of public higher education and the economic status of the state.

In these respects the various state governments differ greatly. To indicate the variations, I have compared forty-eight states on the basis of twelve variables measuring burden, capacity to pay, effort, and

---

11 S. E. Harris, *Higher Education: Resources and Finance* (New York: McGraw-Hill Book Co., 1962), especially chap. 2.

achievements. The burden, for example, is measured by the proportion of college-age population in relation to total population. Grading the states from an A to an E, with the top four an A+ and the bottom four an E, I find that on burden California ranked E+, that is to say, had a relatively low burden, and Texas ranked C+. On capacity, measured by two variables, the first of which is per capita income, the second being net state and local taxes per member of college-age population, California is rated as A+ and Texas as C+. On four criteria of effort, I find that California comes out with a D+ and Texas with a D. In other words, Texas' effort in higher education gets a rather low grade. One index of effort, for example, is state and local taxes per $1,000 of personal income. On four variables measuring achievement, I find that California gets a C and Texas a D. California's low achievement is to some extent misleading. The fact is that California, with its large institutions and numerous students, can produce a college education at relatively low cost, and this contributes to its low achievement grade. In one other respect, a comparison is of some interest. Relatively low-income states tend to find their higher education highly expensive. An explanation of this fact is that as compared to per capita income, the costs of turning out a student are relatively high in low-income states. For this reason I find that Texas comes out with a D, that is, relatively speaking the cost of turning out a student in relation to per capita income is relatively low. In a meaningful sense, Texas matches low per capita income with relatively lower costs per student. For the low-income states, the grade on this criterion is high. Alabama merits an A. In general, the cost of turning out a student in any one year by a public institution can be related to some extent to the size of the state. Where states are relatively small, they tend to have relatively small economies, and their unit costs tend to be high not only in higher education but in many other categories of expenditures.[12]

Institutions that especially depend on endowments are also likely to be in trouble. The contribution of endowment to higher-education income has dropped from about 25 per cent at the beginning of the century to about 5 per cent now. The explanation of this is partly the large increase in other kinds of income; partly the rise in money income which tends to reduce the real purchasing power of the endowment funds and, to some extent, inadequate management of the endowment funds; and partly the great rise in enrollment, for then the contribution of endowment per student tends to decline. Colleges, however, now depend much more on current gifts than they do upon endowment. Tuition tends to play an important part in financing

[12] *Ibid.*, chaps. 26 and 27, especially p. 362.

higher education. There are many who believe that there should be no tuition or minimum fees, and others who hold that the students should be made to pay full cost of the education. Because of differential income gains accruing to college-educated members now on the labor market, estimated at about $100,000 and perhaps $250,000 lifetime income differential for graduates of 1963 (no inflation assumed), a case can be made for charges to the undergraduate. One can, therefore, justify substantial tuition fees on the basis of the financial gains of a college education, though one must not assume that the total differential between what the college student earns and what he would have earned had he not gone to college is to be associated only with his college education. His native ability and environmental factors also are important.

There are others who argue that tuition should be very low on the theory that the nation needs many more college graduates and increased numbers going to college contribute much to the social product. This is, of course, one strong argument for very low tuitions in public institutions. Where public resources are adequate, the case for substantial tuition fees is not strong, but where the state governments can provide the required cash for higher education only if large sacrifices are endured by the taxpayers, and especially by those of low-income groups, the case for high tuition becomes stronger.

An ideal goal would be to charge according to capacity to pay, using large scholarship funds for those able young men and women from low-income groups and high tuition for those who can afford to pay it. This would be an ideal solution were it not for the fact that, according to many college administrators, state legislatures respond to this kind of policy by cutting down their appropriations to higher education. It is clear that the trend in this country is toward more higher education with no or very small fees in the public sector, and it is likely that in the next twenty-five years a much larger part of our population will receive a college education with very low or no tuition at all. Much depends upon the resources available to taxpayers and the attitude of citizens toward higher education, as well as the needs for higher education.

At any rate, if tuition is to increase, a much more generous program of scholarships and of loans should be associated with this higher tuition. In a recent period of about twenty years, tuition increased from $200 million to $1,162 million. This increase would have been difficult to achieve without seriously changing the structure of the student body if student aid had not increased by about ten times.

Loan financing is also highly important in financing of students and is increasing at a very rapid rate. In many respects it would be preferable for parents to invest on behalf of the child beginning at age one. This would be a very effective way of bringing about an improvement in the financing of higher education. The advantage of putting aside a sum of money at age one would be that yield would work on behalf of the student rather than against him, as is true with loan financing. In this age of consumer credit there is a good deal to be said for the use of credit for providing a college education. Two advantages especially are worth mentioning. The first is that under a loan system the burden of financing higher education is shifted, to some extent, to the general population. As incomes rise partly as the result of inflation and partly from rising productivity, the burden of financing the loan is greatly reduced. Secondly, through the use of credit, higher education arrogates to itself an increased proportion of the flow of resources, just as the automobile and housing industries through the use of credit accomplish the same objective.

Finally, there is the problem of cutting down the cost of higher education without deteriorating the quality. It is hard to believe that we could not prune 10 to 20 per cent from the higher-education budget through more efficient and effective use of resources. Since 1890 the cost per resident student has risen by about 900 per cent, an increase way beyond the rise of prices. To some extent this increase in unit costs is explained by the improvement in the quality of the product and the rising standard of living of the American people. The very marked rise in the cost per student has occurred despite the fact that the largest rises in enrollment have prevailed in relatively inexpensive curriculums, such as undergraduate schools of education and business, and junior colleges. The high-cost operations, such as medical schools, play a much smaller part in the total picture. Moreover, the average number of students per institution of higher learning has increased during this period eight or more times, and this also should bring about large economies of scale.

Vis-à-vis per capita income, educational income per resident student has declined. In other words, higher education has not kept up with the general economy. Undoubtedly one explanation of the rising costs of education is related to the fact that the curriculum is under the control of the faculty. The budget is under the control of the administration, but to some extent the demands of the faculty for curriculum changes, a rising number of courses, and small classes tend to increase the budgetary pressures. Higher education suffers from the excessive number of small courses; inadequate use of plants; excessive duplication of facilities; inadequate planning of location; unwillingness to experiment with new teaching methods; and excessive expenditures on fringe educational products such as athletics and public relations. Since I have spelled out all these details of income and expenditures, as well as wastes of higher education in a rather long book, I shall not dwell on them here.[13]

MEDICINE

I now turn to medicine. From 1950 to 1962 the estimated expenditures on medicine grew from $12 to $31 billion, of which the total increase for private outlays was from $9 to $23.5 billion, and for public from $3.3 to $7.6 billion. Since the GNP rose less than 100 per cent in this period, it is easy to see that the proportionate rise in expenditures for health was much more than in the GNP.

Why this large increase in medical outlays? To some extent, of course, the rise reflects general inflation and the rising standard of living of the American people. Improved education and greater awareness of the value of medical service and the rising availability of insurance stimulate rising outlays on medicine. Another relevant factor is an increased surplus of income after covering the costs of other necessaries of life. On top of this, there has been, of course, in the last ten to fifteen years a large increase in the services available. But a large factor in rising expenditures was an increase in the cost of medicine, much beyond that for all prices and even beyond that for prices of all services.

It has sometimes been said that the free market for medical services under which medicine operates in this country has been more successful than the socialized system in Great Britain. The evidence offered for this is that since 1948 the percentage of GNP spent for medicine has risen in the United States and declined in Great Britain. But this is an oversimplification of the problem. Actually if the U.S. GNP and medical expenditures are corrected for relevant rises of prices, and similarly in Great Britain, it will be found that on this basis the record in Great Britain has been better than in the United States. Furthermore, it is well to remember that in Great Britain the relatively small increase in expenditures for medicine is partly a matter of priorities set up by the government. The government gave higher priorities to defense, housing, and education than to medicine. Moreover, in view of the inflationary problem and the unfortunate bal-

13 *Ibid.*; J. D. Millett, *Financing Higher Education in the United States* (New York: Columbia University Press, 1952); S. J. Mushkin, *Economics of Higher Education* (Washington: U.S. Department of Health, Education, and Welfare, 1962); U.S. Department of Health, Education, and Welfare, Office of Education, "Expenditures and Property," in *History of Higher Education, 1957–58* (Washington: 1960); U.S. Department of Health, Education, and Welfare, *Financial Statistics of Institutions of Higher Education, 1959–60* (September, 1962).

ance-of-payments problem, the British government was not prepared to build needed hospitals.

Another relevant factor is that between 1948 and 1960 the income of physicians in the United States rose 2.5 times as much as in Great Britain. In order to get an increase in income, the medical profession in Britain had to justify it by tying it to the rising cost of living and the pay made available to other professions with similar training. Actually, even in Great Britain the income of doctors is about 50 per cent more than the average of other professions. In the United States the average income of a practicing physician is about three times as much as that of the average college professor, but in Great Britain it is only 25 per cent more than that of the college teacher. Such restraint imposed on the income of physicians, of course, tends to keep down the total expenditures on medicine in Great Britain.

Again under British National Health Service (NHS), the British have kept expenditures on drugs down. There is much pressure on physicians to use standard rather than the more expensive proprietary drugs. Physicians who are responsible for very large relative expenditures for drugs are called in for explanations. Furthermore, there is much pressure to avoid excessive differentiation of product, which increases the unit cost and does not add much to the quality of the product.

Perhaps one of the most important factors accounting for the large rise of medical expenditures in the United States has been the great spread of insurance. At the present time, insurance finances about 28 per cent of the total medical expenditures in the United States. On a rather optimistic assumption I estimate that this figure might rise to 43 per cent in ten years. It will not be easy to achieve such an extension of coverage, first because those who are not now covered are the most difficult ones to enroll. They include the unemployed, the old, Negroes, those living in rural communities, and finally (inclusive of the others mentioned) those who are not attached to the labor market. Moreover, the benefits still uncovered, e.g., drugs, are those that require much administration and lend themselves to great abuses. At present, the major coverage is of hospital stay and medical services while in the hospital. Coverages of ordinary visits to physicians, dental services, and drugs are still matters that require a considerable amount of innovation and when offered are likely to bring a great deal of overutilization. The average consumer of medical services is not so likely to restrain himself from using expensive services if they do not involve any substantial additional payment by the patient. Doctors often find it convenient to send patients to the hospital because this facilitates payment of bills or because they are rid of troublesome responsibilities. Since the hospital is likely to provide services covered by insurance, and outside services are not so fully covered, there is a tendency to use hospitals disproportionately.

Another troublesome point about insurance is that those companies which use the non-profit type of insurance like Blue Cross, which provides community rates, that is, equal rates irrespective of risks, are being squeezed out by insurance companies who apply experience rating, that is, who insure on the basis of the likely cost of medical services for the insured. Insurance rates rise steadily and faster than the costs of the covered service. Greater utilization of covered services, related in part to the fact of insurance, but in part also to under-utilization experienced under the fee-for-service approach, is the basic reason why insurance prices have been increasing faster than the costs of the covered services.

One of the most troublesome points in American medicine is the rising cost of hospital care. Whereas the price of medical services in recent years has risen twice as much as the general price level, hospital care has risen twice as much as the cost of all medical services. From 1948 to 1961 private expenditures for hospital care have increased from $1.7 billion to $5.8 billion, and the daily cost of hospital beds has been rising at a galloping rate. In 1960 hospital room rates were about four and a half times as high as they had been in 1940.

Why a rise of such proportions? One factor in the rise is undoubtedly the increased utilization associated with insurance. Here there is a conflict between the interest of hospitals and the national welfare. With excess capacity, hospitals tend to encourage utilization, whereas from the viewpoint of the national economy, this overutilization is wasteful because it tends often unnecessarily to increase the number of beds. Another factor of great importance is the large increase in wage rates in hospitals as well as the substantial rise in the number of personnel in relation to the number of patients. The latter is related to increased services, which are very often expensive. National rises in wage rates influence hospital rates, but increases have been much greater in hospitals where wage rates had been abnormally low. In periods of high employment, the underprivileged and exploited labor elements tend to receive large wage increases. Another factor that accounts for the large hospital expenditures is the increase in new and expensive services. We have come to a point now where a large part of the total hospital bill, sometimes as much as one-half, is not for room and board and routine medical care, but for the special services that are required. A final factor is the point that with insurance paying a large part of the total hospital bill, roughly about 70 per cent today, there is not the careful scrutiny of hospital expenses that there would be if the patient had to make payment directly, as in the past.

From the viewpoint of the national economy, one important waste in medical service is the excessive use of hospitals when less expensive care could be had elsewhere, for example, at home or in a nursing home. Even under the Hill-Burton Act, which provided a large number of additional hospitals, the tendency has been to increase the number of general hospital beds, which on the whole were more nearly adequate, and to neglect beds for psychiatric patients, chronic patients, and patients in nursing homes—all three greatly undersupplied.

In discussing the rise in prices of hospital services, one reservation must be made. The increase in costs seems especially large if the item being measured is the cost per day at the hospital. But a dramatic change in hospital care in the last generation has been a substantial reduction in the number of days per admission. This means that in order to achieve a given cure it takes much less time on the average than it did before. At least to some extent this offsets the rising price of hospital services per day. But even here a counter reservation is necessary. What happens today is that on the average patients in hospitals are afflicted with less-serious illnesses than ten, twenty, or thirty years ago. In this sense, the rise in the cost of a hospital stay is higher than it seems to be, because the average service is a less costly one than it was a number of years ago, when the patients, on the average, had more-serious illnesses. For example, most mothers have their babies in the hospital, whereas twenty-five years ago a large proportion did not. Insurance also tends to bring people to the hospital who would not ordinarily have gone to the hospital.

This whole discussion raises another interesting problem. That problem is the inadequacy of our index numbers for measuring the price of medical services. Might it not be helpful if we could build a new index number which is based on the cost of treating a particular disease and then, perhaps through proper weighting, all diseases? A number of suggestions along these lines have been made in the past.

Clearly an important factor in the rising price of medicine has been the increased income of physicians. *Medical Economics* estimates that the average net income of a practicing physician is about $25,000 today. The explanation of the very large increase in physicians' incomes since before the war lies in the following items listed in order of importance: (1) improved collections, (2) more services per physician, (3) higher prices per service, (4) reduced overhead cost. Should one examine, for example, the index number of the rise of prices of physicians, one would find from 1940 roughly a doubling of income for general practitioners and a rise of about 60 per cent for surgeons' fees. These increases are not out of line when compared with the rise in the general price level, but they may be misleading. With the large increase in the number of specialists in recent years, the average income of the specialist, which thirty years ago was 150 per cent above that of the general practitioner, has now been cut to about 25 per cent above, and this to some extent explains the smaller rise of surgeons' fees. Among physicians, the obstetricians especially have done well, and this is explained by the unusual demand for their services.

But the increase in the price of general practitioners' services may be larger than is indicated by the index numbers. We know now that they perform about twice as many services as they did in the past. Moreover, they require that the patient travel to the doctor rather than the reverse, and this means a deterioration of service. This larger rise in the number of services per week per physician, an increase which can be estimated at 100 per cent, is explained in part by better use of excess capacity; in part by more effective use of the medical team, that is, a larger proportion of nurses, technicians and the like; and finally by a reduction in the number of minutes per visit. The last may or may not suggest a deterioration of the product. Considering all of these factors, the rise in prices per service has certainly been greater than that suggested by the index number.

In one sense there is a free market for the services of physicians because their incomes increase in response to rising demand. In another sense the market is an imperfect one. In response to rising demand and higher incomes there should be a corresponding increase in the number of physicians. But this has been made very difficult by the high cost of building medical schools and the inadequacy of space and also by the opposition—until very recently—of the American Medical Association to any intervention on the part of the government in providing additional space in medical schools. The result is that of the large amount of additional funds which flow into the medical markets, the doctors gain a disproportionate share, compared to other members of the medical team whose response to rising incomes is much greater than that of physicians. Messrs. M. Friedman and S. Kuznets said a long time ago that the differential income of physicians in relation to dentists was much more than could be justified by extra costs of preparation.[14] The differential earnings of the professions today suggest that this statement has even greater validity for physicians at the present time.

One of the objections of the medical profession to the growth of insurance, and especially comprehensive or governmental insurance,

[14] M. Friedman and S. Kuznets, *Income from Independent Professional Practice* (New York: National Bureau of Economic Research, 1945), pp. 118, 127, 390–91.

has been the fear that the doctors would be deprived of the fee-for-service method of payment. There is no doubt that the fee-for-service method results in excessive services, in the same way that salary payments for physicians may well result in inadequate service. In the British system, the physicians compromised and accepted a capitation system, under which a doctor's income depends on the number of patients on his list. Under this system there is the incentive of providing good service in trying to get a larger number of patients, although even under this system there is the tendency to pass on responsibility to specialists, hospitals, and the like.

It is interesting that in the United States the proportion of doctors being paid on a salary basis tends to increase at a fairly rapid rate. This does not necessarily reflect the fact that doctors prefer payment by salary, though their opposition to compensation on a salary basis is not as great as it is sometimes held to be. The explanation is largely that there are many more doctors in the medical schools and hospitals and working for the government.

Another troublesome aspect of medicine is the high cost of drugs. In 1960, drugs (including appliances) accounted for 26 per cent of the medical dollar. Yet from 1940 to 1960, according to the official index number, the price of drugs rose by less than 50 per cent. But there is some question about this index number also. In the first place the weighting has been inadequate and adjustment too tardy. For a long time the index included only aspirin and milk of magnesia as representative of all non-prescription drugs. The adjustment of the index number to the rising importance of proprietary drugs and especially antibiotics has been most delayed. One reason for the moderate increase in the price of drugs has been the fact that with the large development of such drugs as antibiotics, the immediate effect is to introduce some of these drugs into the index number during their experimental stage, when their prices are very high. As their prices are gradually reduced, the effect is to depress the index number or at least to contain its rise.

In a sense, the drug industry is a semipublic utility industry. Yet it reveals the largest profits in relation to capital or sales of any industry. It adheres to many monopolistic practices, for example, identical bids for governmental orders; much lower prices in many foreign countries than in the United States; excessive amount of differentiation of products where there is no realistic differentiation, though the effect is higher unit prices; and tremendous selling expenditures. In many respects the cost structure of the drug industry reminds one of the soap and tobacco industries, where labor costs are relatively small, and advertising and selling costs are remarkably high. In defense of the drug industry it can be said that it provides much research money, although the amount is small compared to total gross receipts.

What are the solutions to the medical problem? The United States government has suggested insurance under OASDI for the old. The approach does not appeal to the medical profession because of a fear that this may be the entering wedge to national compulsory health insurance. I, myself, cannot believe that there is nearly as much chance of national health insurance as there was in the late 1940's, when private insurance had not progressed very far. The influence of the various insurance groups and the American Medical Association is a strong barrier to national health insurance. It may well be that where insurance coverage is most inadequate, that is, for the old, coverage by OASDI might reduce the pressure for a national health insurance program. The American Medical Association, however, takes a somewhat different view of this.

Other measures are necessary. It is important that the insurance companies, that is, the voluntary prepayment companies, make better provisions for those who are not able to afford high-cost insurance. An old person with an average income of a little more than $1,000 cannot afford to pay $300 to cover necessary needs through insurance. It was hoped at one time that private comprehensive prepayment insurance would be the solution to the problem, but this has not been the case. The early opposition of the medical societies and the difficulty of raising capital and of finding policyholders who could afford to pay the $300 or so that was necessary for a really comprehensive insurance program—these have made the spread of private comprehensive insurance very difficult. The Blue Cross, confronted with the competition of insurance companies that, unlike Blue Cross, charge on the basis of likely costs, is gradually losing its share of the market.

Perhaps the best compromise between what is generally called socialized medicine and the present system would be the coverage of the old under some kind of governmental program, and (or) state or federal subsidies for those who cannot afford to pay the full costs of a fairly comprehensive program. A subsidy program encouraging comprehensive prepayment insurance might therefore be most helpful.

Also of much importance would be an increase in the number of medical schools and the output of physicians and members of other health professions. It has been estimated that there is a need for about 50 per cent more medical graduates by 1975 in order to maintain the present patient-doctor ratio. Only through a larger supply of doctors will physicians be spared the embarrassment of an excessively high income which is a source of resentment by others. In the hospital field there are many possibilities of economies and ways of reducing over-utilization. I cannot go into these in this brief paper. Much can be done to improve the free market operations in the drug industry, for example, enlistment of antitrust measures and better control of selling methods by the drug industry.[15]

Conclusions

At the outset I discussed the considerations that determine the allocation of resources for welfare. Here I need add only a few conclusions to be drawn from the discussion of the two major categories, education and health.

It is clear that expenditures for all levels of education continue their steep ascent. The additional burden falls primarily on government Because of the varying tax potentials, much of the responsibility is being transferred from local to state governments, and the pressure is increasingly directed to the federal government. But for various reasons, the contribution of the federal government has been kept at a minimum—aside from payments for services rendered, e.g., research in higher education—the private sector is still a major factor. But even here, the competition of the public institutions of higher learning threatens to reduce the relative contribution of private schools by at least one-half, from 50 per cent in 1950, to 25 per cent by 1975.

In health, the major problem is strengthening the financial institutions in such a manner that insurance would cover at least 50 per cent of all medical costs and have a coverage of people close to 100 per cent. Whereas, in education, capacity to profit is a condition for use, a view widely held is that *all* are entitled to medical care. We are far from that position today. Voluntary insurance has already greatly improved the distribution of medical services among people of varying economic status. But coverage of less than 30 per cent of costs is not enough. The road to an adequate medical program is greater recourse to insurance as a mechanism for diverting resources to medicine, improving their distribution, and reducing costs of services insofar as these are performed uneconomically or yield rewards that greatly exceed what is necessary to obtain manpower of adequate quality. Failure to achieve these objectives greatly increases the threat of government intervention—the government already spends $7 billion for medical care.

[15] A vast literature is devoted to medical economics. See especially Herman M. Somers and Anne R. Somers, *Doctors, Patients, and Health Insurance* (Washington: The Brookings Institution, 1961); M. M. Davis, *Medical Care for Tomorrow* (New York: Harper & Bros., 1955); A. Lindsey, *Socialized Medicine in England and Wales* (Chapel Hill, N.C.: University of North Carolina Press, 1962); and S. E. Harris, *Economics of American Medicine* (New York: Macmillan Co., 1963).

JACOB VINER

The United States as a "Welfare State"

I PLAN in my lecture to compare the pattern or "style" of the present-day American economy with earlier patterns here and elsewhere
and with currently prevailing patterns elsewhere. To do so I must
make use of abstract and ambiguous labels for different kinds of economic systems, much as I would prefer to be able to dispense with
them. There are only three other alternatives that I can conceive of,
and none of these is a practicable one. I could make use of a set of
labels which are not abstract, which have precise and uniform meaning regardless of time or country, and which have the quality of automatically and accurately communicating that meaning to any audience, whether a sophisticated one like the one that is honoring me at
this moment by permitting me to address it or a naïve and simple-
minded one. But such a set of labels does not exist in the field of economics or of any of the social science disciplines. Or I could dispense
with labels and each time that I refer to a particular economic system
or pattern repeat the full inventory of its fundamental characteristics.
Or I could do so only upon first reference to a particular system,
thereafter using such colorless and un-mnemonic symbols as System
A, System B, and so forth. Either of these latter procedures would
lead to intolerable boredom for you, and perhaps also for myself.
There is therefore no escape from the use of labels too simple and un-
informative for the ideas they are intended to communicate.

In controversial fields, however, labels in the course of the history
of their use inevitably lose some of the objectivity they may have
had when originally invented and become carriers of undertones of
praise or blame, thus becoming substitutes for rational thought instead of its tools. These undertones, moreover, are liable to be ran-
dom and undisciplined and to vary with the period, the region, and
the persons using them or hearing them used. The greatest of the

JACOB VINER is Walker Professor of Economics, Emeritus, at Princeton University.

risks connected with the use of labels is that when a speaker intends one undertone to be caught by his audience, the audience will catch a different one. I know no way whereby these risks and uncertainties can be completely overcome, and no way but continued and disciplined exchange of views conducted in a spirit of cool and mutually tolerant discourse by which they can be reduced to moderate dimensions. I can only affirm that it is not my purpose on this occasion to persuade or to convert anyone to anything, to comfort anyone, or to antagonize anyone, and that even if such were my purpose I would do my best to confine myself to logical discourse rather than semantic tricks. But words are treacherous tools, and no matter who is pouring them out on you, eternal vigilance is in the last analysis your only effective defense against being betrayed by them. I have at least put you on your guard.

I choose as a convenient label for the present-day pattern or style of organization of the American economy "the welfare state." The term is of German origin and seems first to have been used in the 1870's by German economists as a term of praise for the social goals of Bismarck and the legislation he was initiating to promote them. With substantial similarity in meaning it is being widely used today to describe the existing or the desired pattern of economic organization in the industrialized countries this side of the Iron Curtain. It is fairly frequently used as a label for the American economic pattern as it has evolved especially since the initiation of the New Deal, although in the United States other labels are sometimes preferred: for example, "people's capitalism," "welfare capitalism," "the mixed economy," and, by critics on the right, the "mixed-up economy" and "cryptosocialism"; by critics on the left, "monopoly capitalism," "decadent capitalism," "Madison Avenue capitalism," and, as the most recent derogatory term to obtain wide currency, the "affluent society." The purport of this last term seems to be to associate with our notions of the quality of our existing system the depressing idea that under it all classes have more income even after taxes than they know how to spend wisely and yet refuse to let the government decide for them the choice between the available range of commodities and services which their incomes shall be used to procure.

It is easier to be precise on what the welfare state is not than on what it is. Like the aristocratic or theocratic societies prior to the Industrial Revolution, and like socialism, communism, fascism, naziism, but in lesser degree than all of these, the welfare state is a rejection of the laissez faire or "liberal" system which substantially prevailed in the Western world in the nineteenth century, and this halfway or partial rejection of laissez faire is, I think, the most uniform and the most important distinguishing mark of the welfare state. By laissez faire is meant, of course, a system under which the intervention of government in economic matters, whether as regulator or operator, is confined to the barest practical minimum consistent with the maintenance of order, the enforcement of contracts, the protection of individuals against direct and overt coercion by other individuals, and the maintenance of the military personnel and facilities necessary for defense against external aggression. In the nineteenth-century liberal society the emphasis was on freedom for the individual from government, not on service to him by government. In the modern forms of authoritarian state the emphasis is on service to the individual, with the character of the service determined from above and with statist coercion substituted for the political and civil freedoms of the liberal society. The welfare state tries to find a middle path between service without freedom and freedom without service.

In the liberal nineteenth-century state rich and poor were in principle equally protected from encroachment on their property rights, their rights to follow the occupation of their choice, to live where they pleased, think and say what they pleased, and spend what they had the means to spend on things of their own untrammeled choice. For the organization of the productive process, for the attainment of equilibrium as between what producers chose to produce and what consumers chose to consume, for the determination of the ratio in which income currently produced should be allocated to current consumption or be saved and invested, reliance was on competitive market forces. That competition left to its own devices might lead to private monopoly was either overlooked or denied or believed to be adequately guarded against if government itself refrained from establishing or promoting private monopoly power and enforced the common-law prohibitions of overt conspiracy in restraint of trade.

Wealth always brings to its possessors power and privilege. The privileges which the rich specially enjoyed under laissez faire, however, were for the most part not privileges conferred upon them by government but arose directly or indirectly out of their possession of sufficient wealth to buy such things as education, medical services, gracious mansions, leisure, art, and mistresses. The most ambitious, the most intelligent and gifted, the most lucky of the working classes succeeded in increasing numbers, but for the most part without substantial assistance from government, in acquiring moderate shares in these material means to the good life, and many of these rose into the ranks of a rapidly growing middle class, which was eventually to impose on most of the Western countries the substitution of democratic political institutions for the absolutist or the aristocratic regimes of the past.

In the nineteenth century average incomes appear to have risen impressively in all of the Western countries, although there is a great scarcity of reliable statistical information. But this increase in average income was in Europe at least in large part and perhaps wholly the result of the relative rise in the size of the middle classes as compared with the working classes. The lower classes gained from the progress of technology some improvement in health and in mortality and some improvement in the lighting and heating of their homes. On the other side of the ledger for them, however, were the increasing congestion and the decreasing access to sun and air and light in their homes, and apparently also deterioration in the quality of the food they ate and the clothes they wore. As best I can determine, it was not until about the 1870's that it can be said with assurance that the standard of living of the bottom 50 per cent of the population of any western or northern European country was clearly and substantially higher than it had been in, say, 1820 or 1750 or 1650 or perhaps even 1550. It was not, I think, chiefly political democracy that brought the genuine improvement which did occur from the 1870's on, but largely the cheaper and better food from North America, the Argentine, Australia, and New Zealand which the application of steam to ocean and land transport made available to western Europe, and the decline in the working-class birth rate which resulted from the widespread resort to birth-control practices beginning in the 1870's.

Political democracy, laissez faire, and the persistence of mass poverty for the working classes while above them were conspicuous expenditure and growing accumulated wealth—these together constituted an unstable mixture which could not last. It gave rise to socialist movements of several species, and it may be that the fact that the latter failed everywhere before World War I to bring about an explosion of the mixture was largely due to the circumstance that the governments of the time were prudent enough to grant the newly enfranchised masses political platforms from which to voice their complaints and that a foretaste of the welfare state, such as the Bismarckian social legislation in Germany and the Lloyd George death duties in England, as well as the growth in strength of the trade unions, opened up vistas of the possibility of reaching the Promised Land by milder means than revolutionary socialism. In any case, the welfare state of today has its roots in the nineteenth-century dissatisfaction of the working classes with the workings of laissez faire capitalism. The welfare state also constitutes a partial rejection of the alternatives to laissez faire which nineteenth-century socialist movements proposed. Let me now turn to a more positive description of the characteristics of the welfare state.

In the welfare state the central and subsidiary governments engage in a wide range of economic activities. They accept responsibility for ironing out the business cycle, for relief of the unemployed, and for an extensive program of cradle-to-grave insurance against the normal hazards of life. They encourage and regulate collective bargaining between employer and employee with respect to wages, hours of labor, and working conditions, usually with what on nineteenth-century criteria is an open and systematic bias in favor of labor. Through progressive tax systems and expenditures directed largely to the subsidization of the low-income sections of the country and sectors of the population, they claim to exercise a strong equalizing influence on the distribution of wealth and income.

With respect to free competition in the market, they are torn between two opposite doctrines: on the one hand, the doctrine that free competition is the most effective stimulus to improvement, leads to the closest approximation of material rewards to social contribution, and maximizes flexibility and adaptability to changes in tastes, processes, and relative abundance of productive factors, the fundamental proposition of nineteenth-century laissez faire liberalism; on the other hand, the doctrine that free competition leads to duplication of facilities and services, to booms and busts, to the crushing of the weak by the strong, and eventually to private monopoly. They thus embark on extensive and improvised rather than precisely designed programs of governmental intervention. These programs leave a large measure of freedom to market forces and to individual initiative—or lack of it—but they involve a wide range of activities of a regulatory or supervisory character. These programs include also many types of more direct participation by government in economic activity, including even some measure of substitution of government for private operation of industry. Selected industries, especially agriculture, are shielded from the full rigors of competitive forces by subsidization, price supports, preferential tax treatment, and government stockpiling.

The volume and allocation of capital formation are deliberately influenced by subjection of capital issues on the market to licensing, by setting up governmental credit agencies which increase the availability of capital at low rates for selected industries by direct lending of government funds, and by guarantees of repayment to private lenders, the industries so favored being selected on the basis of a variety of social policies and political grounds, but always in response to special concern for the prosperity of particular sectors of the population. In the United States, for example, agriculture, the housing needs of the low-income classes, small business, and ocean shipping are given special favors, and here, as in other welfare-state countries, decaying industries and new pioneer industries are given aid to the recovery of strength or to its new acquisition.

In response to special needs or to political strength, the welfare state typically deals ambivalently with monopolistic practices; in some sectors it combats them by antitrust and anticartel legislation; in other sectors it sanctions and even enforces them, as (to take the United States as an example) in the case of agriculture, in the sanction of price maintenance in the field of retail distribution, and, above all, with respect to labor-union practices. "Natural monopolies" such as railroads, urban mass-transportation facilities, electricity and gas generation and distribution, dock facilities, bridges, and roads are either owned and operated by governmental agencies or are closely controlled as to rates and quality of service by government. But this feature of the welfare state is in the main but a moderate extension of the "municipal socialism" which became common from the 1870's on as the working classes won a greater measure of political power. "Nationalization" of industry outside the area of public utilities is not a prominent feature of the welfare state, and its substantial absence from program and practice today is perhaps the most important fact justifying the drawing of a sharp distinction between even the democratic socialism of the nineteenth century and the present-day welfare state. In the welfare state education is made widely available, is overwhelmingly conducted in governmental institutions, and when left in private hands is usually both substantially financed and closely regulated by government.

To finance their activities and also to make taxation serve as an instrument for redistribution of the national income, welfare states collect in taxes up to 30 per cent or more of the national income. Income taxes are invariably steeply progressive and taxes on business are heavy, and in general the total effect of the tax and expenditure activities of the welfare state is probably in a significant degree such as to make the national pattern of income distribution a less unequal one than it would be if all tax revenues were derived from a proportional tax on income and if all governmental expenditures in their immediate impact bestowed benefits on individuals in conformity with the over-all pattern of national distribution of income. But all the welfare states have democratic processes of government including universal suffrage; in all of them the middle classes and those of the lower-income groups who have absorbed "bourgeois" attitudes are a great and often preponderant portion of the total population, and welfare-state politicians, like all politicians, are highly sensitive to strategically located and well-organized aggregates of voting power. The welfare state is consequently nowhere exclusively and rarely predominantly a "proletarian" state. It is often, at least intermittently, a "bourgeois" or middle-class-dominated state. In consequence, whatever its proclaimed program of income equalization may be, its tax bite is rarely as strong as its tax bark. Even when income- and inheritance-tax rate schedules are in appearance progressive to the point of near expropriation of the high-bracket incomes or estates, they are invariably accompanied by an elaborate set of loopholes which temper the tax winds for the partially shorn sheep.

Government subsidies, moreover, do not flow exclusively to the very poor, and even though predominantly it is rich Peters who are taxed to pay poor Pauls, to a substantial extent the net outcome of the complex tax-and-subsidy system is that Peter is taxed to pay Peter, after deduction of an appropriate charge to reimburse the government for its services in keeping the taxpayers' money in circulation. In the welfare state instances are even to be found where the very comfortably well-off succeed in one way or another in getting on the dole in forms and dimensions which add to the social status of the recipient instead of, as in the case of poor relief, detracting from it. To a liberal or to an old-fashioned Socialist, this may seem a funny way to run a country, but it is a significant characteristic of the welfare state that it is essentially a democratic response to the whole range of popular interests, values, and aspirations, and that in consequence its general pattern is bound to lack complete internal coherence and to display to the scrutinizing eye instances of gross inconsistency.

To conservatives of the American type, this concern of mine with the selection of an appropriate label for our present-day economic system would probably seem superfluous trifling with the obvious, since the century-old term "socialism" would adequately serve all purposes, or at least all *their* purposes, and a fresh label would not lessen the menace of the poison. I would not only concede but would emphasize that the modern welfare state embodies substantial elements of nineteenth-century democratic socialism. I would even concede the reasonableness of applying to it some such label as "new socialism" or "neosocialism," or even "twentieth-century democratic socialism," provided it were conceded that "new capitalism" or "neo-capitalism" would not be an appreciably more misleading term for it and provided it is not claimed that there are no important differ-

ences between the programs of nineteenth-century socialist movements and the practices of present-day welfare states.

Nineteenth-century socialism in all of its variants was the doctrine
of groups out of power and with no early prospects of power. The
orthodox Marxian Socialists had a doctrine of criticism of the capitalism of their time and a program of revolutionary overturn of it
by an elite acting on behalf of, though not itself members of, the
proletariat. Marx and his most loyal disciples carefully refrained from
spelling out any of the details of social organization that would be
introduced "come the Revolution." To what extent this was the
result of utopian dreaming, as the proposition that under socialism
"the state would wither away" suggests, or was strategic concealment
of firm intentions, is still a matter of debate among both friendly and
hostile students of the sacred Marxian texts. But from the Marxian
critique of nineteenth-century liberal capitalism we have every right
to infer that the Marxian aspirations included the complete abolition
of private property in the tools of production, a regime under which
all able-bodied adults would have to work if they wanted to eat, and
suppression of the allegedly sham freedom of political democracy.

The present-day practices of the welfare state do not conform to
any of these three goals, and with a minor qualification with respect
to nationalization with which I will deal later, none of these is given
a place in any welfare-state program I know anything about. Marxian
socialism also had a decided equalitarian bias, and "from each according to his capacity and to each according to his needs" sounds clearly
to my ears like an equalitarian slogan even if I don't claim to know
what it means or for that matter what "equality" as a rule for distribution of income would mean in precise terms. I am sure of one
thing, that in the heaven of original Marxianism or in the present-day
Communist version of it as it operates in Russia and elsewhere, the
rule of equality closely resembles the leaden Lesbian architectural
rule which Aristotle speaks of which adapted itself to every bend
or curvature of a wall that appealed to the designing architect's
fancy or judgment. In the present-day welfare state there is no doubt
a widespread belief in the virtue of "equalization" of income if that
is interpreted to mean the gradual elimination of extremes both of
wealth and of poverty. Beyond this, I see no clear signs of more
ambitious plans or of more radical practice. The welfare state is a
threat to the top 10 (or perhaps 5) per cent of its population in terms
of the amounts of wealth or disposable income after taxation they
will be allowed to retain, and a promise, a realized one in a number
of countries, for the lowest 10 or perhaps 20 per cent of the population, in terms of the minimum standard of living that will be guar-

anteed to them. This may be good or it may be bad, but it is a far cry from Marxian socialism.

Let me now compare the present-day welfare state with non-Marxian nineteenth-century socialist philosophy, although this is to compare a working system without a philosophy with a philosophy which never had the responsibility of application, and whose many and highly changeable programs were therefore more directed toward harvesting votes than drawing up blueprints for whose practicality they had need to worry about. All the nineteenth-century democratic-socialist movements, however, did emphasize "nationalization" of the facilities and instruments of production and a large measure of equalization of income. Such proposals retain a place in the formal programs of some important socialist parties which today operate in welfare states and which are or have been in power. But there is no evidence that outside their minority left wings there is any serious intent on the part of these "socialist" parties actively to pursue these goals, and there is abundant and growing evidence that the present trend of democratic-socialist thought is to abandon these goals as obsolete, as unnecessarily extreme, and as a menace to the political success of the socialist parties in election campaigns.

What seems to have happened is that the socialist party leaders have realized that the middle classes who are terrified by the preaching of such goals are steadily growing in numbers, that political power cannot be maintained or attained unless large numbers can be won over from among the middle classes to their ranks, and that the wage earners themselves are reasonably content with the progress they have made despite the absence of nationalization and of radical equalization; that these latter have not found their status or income or incentives or working conditions appreciably improved when the government has substituted itself for the capitalist as their employer, and indeed that they have in large part absorbed the values and the attitudes of the middle classes and cannot be depended on to continue to give loyal support to parties calling themselves "socialist" or "labor" if these actually and vigorously pursue extreme policies.

Part of the loss of zeal within the socialist parties for fargoing equalization of incomes as a major goal stems from a newly acquired disposition to recognize that in any social system income differentials are essential elements of an adequate set of incentives to effort, to acquisition and exercise of skill, and to assumption of managerial responsibilities. Increasingly also there is belief even among Socialists for whom the idea of "equality" has great moral appeal that as a fact of life the maintenance and expansion of a cultural elite, the promotion of creative art, and the skilled and dedicated diffusion of its fruits do or may require that special material incentives be provided for gifted persons to develop their capacities, and that the conditions of their working life must for such persons be made easier and more removed from discomfort, enforced toil, and responsibilities for family support, than for the ordinary run of worker. Important also has been the realization, with the growth and improvement in quality of statistics of income, of how modest the improvement in economic status of the poorer 50 per cent of the population would be in most countries if there were divided equally among it the wealth, or the wealth and income, in excess of the national average of, say, the richer 50 per cent of the population.

While these socialist or labor parties have consequently been moving visibly toward the right in philosophy and in action, all but extreme wings of the parties right of center have been moving toward the center or perhaps even beyond it. Party affiliations are, of course, more closely tied up with class structure in the European welfare states than in the United States or Canada and are emotionally bound to historical traditions of passionate participation in major struggles for principle and for power; interclass mobility is much less free in Europe than in this country, except that in this country racial and religious barriers are important. Party distinctions, therefore, mean more and are more stable in Europe than here, and I am not claiming that because the parties there are moving closer to each other there is real prospect that the distinctions between them in goals and attitudes will cease to be important. All that I claim is that except for extreme wings of small size and limited range, all the major democratic political parties in Europe operate well within the limits of tolerance of the welfare state and that no threat exists (France perhaps excepted and for other reasons than purely economic issues) of violent social strife in these countries in the absence of subversion by agents of external forces.

The parties of the left which continue to call themselves socialist may or may not be justified in doing so. In most European countries, as in almost all underdeveloped countries, it seems to be good strategy for a political party to carry a "socialist" or "social" label. In the United States and in Canada, on the other hand, it seems clear that it would be political suicide. But whatever labels modern political parties of the left adopt for themselves, all the major parties of the left in the welfare states differ in important respects in programs, in attitudes, in convictions, and in their practice when they gain power from the socialist parties of pre–World War I of which they are the historical heirs. They are not revolutionaries even when political victory by democratic process seems to be beyond their reach, and they are not authoritarians, or prone to engage in large-scale nationalization, or radical equalizers of income, even when they do gain power. They are constitutional parties, and they know, or believe, that their strength would evaporate if they showed signs of losing faith in democratic process and in the adequacy of persuasion by argument and exhortation as the means whereby to retain and to augment their strength.

In the underdeveloped countries many socialist parties are, however, quite close in their programs and doctrines to the European socialist philosophy of the nineteenth century. They lack democratic traditions, and the economic and social problems they face seem more serious and less susceptible of solution or even of palliation than the corresponding problems of western Europe today, or even fifty or a hundred years ago. The population problem is for them a major and perhaps incurable problem within a space of time short enough to be tolerated. The mild remedies by which the advanced countries succeeded in eliminating all but minor residues of the plague of desperate mass poverty (which a hundred years ago prevailed in most of Europe nearly as virulently as it does today in much of Asia, Africa, and Latin America) to many observers do not seem to be effective or appropriate in the setting of the underdeveloped countries. Middle classes are small and relatively unimportant in a majority of the underdeveloped countries, and the gulf between the very rich and the very poor is emptier and wider than it ever was in western Europe, to say nothing of the United States and the European-colonized members of the British Commonwealth.

In much of the underdeveloped world violence as an instrument of social change is not held in abhorrence, and democratic processes of making social decisions are either weak and without the backing of long-established traditions and values or are non-existent. Social change by means of violent revolution, of expropriation and confiscation of the property of the rich, of nationalization of existing industry and establishment under government ownership and management of new industry seem to many in these countries and to some of their friends in welfare-state countries to be their only means of escape from deepening misery and total despair.

For this and other reasons the United States has for about a decade been attempting to nudge them, with the assistance of American financial aid and technical guidance, to adopt welfare-state or "moderate" programs as the remedy for their ills. Their problems, however, may be too deep-rooted and the material and human resources available to them too scanty to make moderate reform either in fact or in appearance sufficient to meet in time and degree the minimum demands which the aroused expectations of their masses lead them to press on their governments. The suppression of human rights, the cruelty, the totalitarianism of the Iron Curtain countries do not deeply shock them, for these are evils which for centuries they have learned to live with. Many in these countries are convinced that some of the Communist programs of social change have been effective for the Communist countries and would be effective for them in providing food, health, education, and status for the masses, in reducing to tolerable proportions the gap between rich and poor, and in endowing them with the mass-production factories which have become for them the outstanding marks of successful economic development.

In guarded fashion high officials and distinguished experts in this and other welfare-state countries are of late revealing in what seems to be a growing tide of opinion that they also are becoming convinced that the methods by which prosperity has been attained in Europe and North America are too mild, too slow, too dependent on a rich foundation of accumulated wealth, of natural resources, and of trained personnel to be adequate to cope with the problems facing the underdeveloped countries. It seems clear that to some extent the American government itself is today trying to convert the better-off classes in some of the underdeveloped countries to acceptance of measures encroaching so drastically on traditional property rights that they would be regarded with horror and apprehension if proposed in this country by any responsible person. If newspaper accounts are to be trusted, the adoption of methods of social change which in their radical character go "beyond the welfare state" with respect to permissible procedures is to some extent being made a condition of continued eligibility for American foreign aid. It may be that this is a sign on our part of maturity and of freedom from excessive doctrinairism and of a willingness to perceive and to face uncomfortable facts. As a believer in the great long-run virtues of patterns of due process and of respect for long-established human rights, including property rights, I am, however, very deeply concerned about this, and I feel that there is urgent need for sober and balanced public discussion of the issue, lest we find ourselves committed, when it is too late to retreat, to pushing the underdeveloped countries down a slippery and perilous slope more rapidly than is safe for us or for their peoples.

This may be too pessimistic a view of the prospects that the underdeveloped countries will seek and find cures for their economic and social ills in programs which can be reconciled with democratic processes and with the preservation of some degree of respect for the long-established rights and the willingness and capacity to render valuable services to the common good of a reformed, enlightened, and self-disciplined, propertied middle class. Financial and technical aid from the richer countries, more generous tariff treatment by these countries of the commodities which are and will long continue to be the staple exports of the underdeveloped countries, breakthroughs through research and experiment in the discovery of successful means of adapting to tropical soils, tropical climates, and tropical and semi-tropical cultural patterns of the great stock of scientific and technological knowledge which is at their disposal in the advanced countries or can be made available to them—these may yet serve to make the underdeveloped countries safe for democracy and to make democracy seem to them unqualifiedly safe for themselves. Even more important in my perhaps biased opinion would be the discovery of cheap, simple, and effective methods of birth control whose widespread use would not be prevented by ignorance, by cultural prejudices, and by religious dogmas kept in a frozen state of rigidity and immunized from the processes of "progressive revelation" and of "development" of dogma which for both Protestantism and Catholicism have at critical periods in the social history of mankind been invoked to permit religious faith to serve as a powerful aid to social reform rather than operating as a stubborn and irrational barrier to it.

If I may return to the domestic scene, the United States is about as fully a welfare state now as any other of the advanced and democratic countries, including those like the Scandinavian countries and New Zealand whose regimes, intermittently at least, are in the hands of political parties which bear with pride the socialist label. There are features of the American economic system which are somewhat special to it, but these for the most part do not derive their importance from their relationship to or independence of the philosophies of nineteenth-century non-Marxian socialist movements and their modern heirs. In its ideology the American public, and especially its more conservative sectors, clings more faithfully to the maxims and stereotypes of nineteenth-century laissez faire than do even the European prototypes—if such there be—of the National Association of Manufacturers, the United States Chamber of Commerce, or the American Medical Association. But these are in large part merely semantic loyalties on our part, rather than operative rules for actual behavior. Laissez faire in fact was notoriously not the ruling principle of our captains of industry when it was the tariff that was in issue. This ideological conservatism on our part probably renders us a useful service to some extent, perhaps in preserving for us old elements of policy which deserve to be preserved or to be resuscitated, but most obviously in fostering a scrutinizing and critical inspection by the American public of all proposals for change.

The welfare state is at best a hastily improvised system having characteristics stretching all the way through the range from near-statism to near-anarchy. It is an unplanned response to a host of historical forces and of political pressures which has not yet acquired, and may never acquire, an internally coherent and logically formulated philosophy. It is undergoing constant change, and its movements, forward, backward, and sideways, are not guided by any clear and widely accepted consensus as to where it is going or where it should go from here. It needs critics more than advocates or prophets, and there is applicable to it the saying, "Woe unto Israel if the prophets should ever get the upper hand!" Theodore Roosevelt many years ago thought he perceived a lunatic fringe to every popular movement for reform, but was blind to the fact that there are lunatic fringes on the right as well as the left. But even these fringes, while scarcely ornamental, have some utilitarian services to perform. They press the advocate to seek for good reasons to support the causes he is preaching, and they stimulate the voter to ask the promoter of a new idea to stand up and defend it. Even blind resistance to change increases the probability that the over-all quality of the changes that will be made will be higher than in its absence.

It is not because of a unified and coherent social philosophy that it realizes in practice but rather because under it the working classes are reasonably satisfied with their present status and see substantial promise of improvement in it for their children even when not for themselves that the modern welfare state has strength and capacity for survival. In one of his poems, Robert Frost asks:

> . . . How are we to write
> The Russian novel in America
> As long as life goes on so unterribly?
>
> *(New Hampshire* [1923])

It is not only in America but throughout the free world where the welfare state prevails that there is no prospect and no wish that the "Russian novel" be written. But if in these countries life for the masses was not "unterrible" and if the more fortunate few in these countries showed no compassion for misery and used their power to resist all change, all that would be needed would be the appearance of a demagogic leader to make imminent the danger of a violent social revolution which would make no fine distinctions between the good and the evil in old traditions and institutions and would bring toppling down upon both the well-off and the poor the debris of a social system which through lack of understanding, of sympathy for distress, and of prudence had failed to take the steps necessary if it was to earn and assure its survival.

It is a special characteristic of the American form of welfare state that its political structure makes even more unlikely than for other welfare states close correspondence between a coherent social philosophy and the predominant pattern of social practice. The American system is marked by extreme diffusion of legislative, judicial, and administrative power, and even if consensus of doctrine were almost complete on the part of the public, the machinery for translating this into consistent and co-ordinated practice would be lacking in large degree. There is, first, the "federal" aspect of our constitution, which involves a sharing of ultimate sovereignty between the national government and state governments, with the line of demarcation of powers, though shifting in response to technological change and to the processes of change in the social philosophy of our supreme judiciary, persisting as a barrier to effectively centralized national social planning.

There is, second, the constitutional separation of powers between national executive and national legislature, with much less concentration of power except in major emergencies in the hands of the executive than prevails under the parliamentary forms of government which almost all other welfare states follow, and which brings it about that in the United States there is much greater scope than elsewhere for conflict and deadlock between executive and legislative, and need for much greater resort to *ad hoc* compromise in the processes of formulation and execution of the grand strategy and the day-to-day tactics of policy.

There is, third, the division of power between the Senate and the House of Representatives, which makes their relations a close analogue to the "duopoly" of economic theory where for over a century the best minds in the economic profession have utterly failed to discover a formula which describes realistically the mode whereby the inevitable conflicts of interest and of objectives between the two equal powers obtain resolution.

There is, fourth, the almost promiscuous and haphazard dispersal of power within each branch of the legislature, where the weakness of party discipline and the possession of nearly unlimited veto power and delaying power by the committee chairmen, who acquire their posts by seniority regardless of the degree and quality of their ability, of their loyalty to the President, or of their loyalty to their party, result in the processes of legislation being largely subject to the idiosyncrasies and the special interests of a small group of men whose qualifications for meeting the heavy responsibilities they bear, whether it be qualities of ability or of character, are even more subject to the hazards of chance than the outcome of a horse race or a football match.

There is, fifth, the substantial power of the run-of-the-mill congressman or senator in initiating, delaying, or modifying specific legislative proposals, which results in making extremely difficult and even impossible the attainment of coherence, timeliness, and self-consistency in the legislative processes as a whole and in making unduly important the role of the lobbyist for special interests, private or regional, who to attain his objectives, good or bad, often needs not the approval of the President or of the administration or of the majority party as a whole or of national public opinion or of the press, but only the dedicated and not necessarily disinterested support of a small handful of free-wheeling legislators.

There is, finally, the power of the judiciary, subject to no formal limits except its own standards of judgment and discretion and its own interpretation of its constitutional function and authority, to find *ultra vires* the outcome of the legislative process and even to engage in the equivalent of legislation itself, through its execution of its duty to interpret the intent of Congress and its practice of "filling the gaps" in acts of Congress in the course of its adjudication of specific cases that come before it for decision.

For all these reasons and for additional reasons which limitations of time or of my knowledge and insight prevent me from bringing to your attention, there is in the abstract no reason for making an idol of the welfare state in its American form or for dedicating ourselves unreservedly to its continuance as it is today without qualification or amendment. Given the complex and puzzling problems it is continually facing, the imperfection of the procedures whereby it deals with problems which it cannot evade or defer or with problems which special interests may press upon it for premature resolution, it would be only by the dispensation of a benevolent Providence that it would ever make precisely the right decisions or always avoid major mistakes. It does not have theoretical superiority over all conceivable alternative systems nor ability to register faithfully and accurately the national consensus on every issue that comes before it, on many of which Congress and the President often show that even they had been unaware of just what is wanted and just what should be done until at the termination of the confused and muddled legislative process they examined what they had in fact done. If, therefore, I nevertheless conclude that I believe that the welfare state, like Old Siwash, is really worth fighting for and even dying for as compared to any rival system, it is because, despite its imperfections in theory and in practice, in the aggregate it provides more promise of preserving and enlarging human freedoms, temporal prosperity, the extinction of mass misery, and the dignity of man and his moral improvement than any other social system which has previously prevailed, which prevails elsewhere today, or which, outside Utopia, the mind of man has been able to provide a blueprint for.

A traveler on a main but congested highway said to a local yokel that his map indicated that there were two side roads at that point which were shortcuts to his destination, and asked for advice as to which of the two to shift to. To which the yokel replied: "Whichever of the two you take, mister, you will wish to God that you had taken the other, or neither." That is how I feel about the availability of other paths to the good society than that which the welfare state provides, strewn as that path is with boulders, pitfalls, detours, and unpredictable as is its ultimate terminus.